TEAM SPIRITUALITY

A Guide for Staff and Church

WILLIAM J. CARTER

Abingdon Press
Nashville

TEAM SPIRITUALITY: A GUIDE FOR STAFF AND CHURCH

Copyright © 1997 by Abingdon Press

This book is printed on recycled, acid-free paper.

Library of Congress Cataloging-in-Publication Data

Carter, William.
    Team spirituality : a guide for staff and church / William Carter.
      p. cm.
    Includes bibliographical references.
    ISBN 0-687-01604-5 (pbk.)
    1. Group ministry.   2. Spiritual life—Christianity.   I. Title.
BV675.C37   1997
253—dc20
                                  96-32278
                                    CIP

97 98 99 00 01 02 03 04 05 06 — 10 9 8 7 6 5 4 3 2 1

MANUFACTURED IN THE UNITED STATES OF AMERICA

This book is dedicated to seven women who have helped form my life and ministry. Some of them have been instrumental in the development of this book.

My wife, Belle, who endured it all,
My mother, Orpha, who was faithful to the end,
and:
Joy Carr
Phyllis Hail
Evelyn Laycock
Mary Virginia Taylor
Martha Jean Bratton

FOREWORD

This book has been in progress for many years. During that time I have been involved in staff administration in both local churches and on a denominational level, and for a dozen years I have been conducting multiple-staff workshops and consulting with numerous local churches about staff relationships. Each year I have thought I had it down pat—and each year have discovered that changes in the mood of the Christian community and in the general managerial environment have made me rethink what I was doing and saying. Working with staffs is a dynamic, evolving process that will continue to challenge all those who feel called to exercise their gifts in a collective ministry to the Body of Christ.

I have learned much from the staff members of the churches and agencies that have been my home for twenty-five years. Early on I discovered that many of them knew more about the church, and about administration, than I did. It also became apparent that a lot of negotiation was necessary to find successful ways of working together. Eventually they became my family, my support group, and a spiritual resource. I wish I could mention each one by name. Every one has been both associate and mentor.

The Intentional Growth Center at Lake Junaluska, North Carolina, and its director, James Warren, gave me a place to collect my thoughts. Each year I taught two seminars on multiple-staff administration at the center, which led to other opportunities to teach and consult. I visited a number of denominational and independent congregations to ask questions. Although there are a number of excellent books about local church staff administration, I began to feel there might be room for a basic book on theology and practice that could be used by administrators, staff members, and personnel committees as a guide for developing a more effective team ministry. The writing began five years ago, a chapter a year. Finally I sent four chapters to Abingdon Press. The editor of professional books decided to take a chance—and this is the result.

Although the original manuscript included a chapter on spirituality, it was the editor who helped me focus on that topic as a unifying theme for the manuscript. Without him and his colleagues the chapters might never have become a book at all. The biblical background and basic administrative processes came together when they were directed toward the development of team spirituality.

Only passing references are made to management theories. I am certain that new administrative techniques will have emerged by the time this book is distributed. As with those in current favor I will recommend them as means to an enlivened ministry and a more exciting personal life. But I feel that there is a fundamental drive to the ministry of word and deed that transcends all methodology and individual techniques. It is to that union of the mind of Christ and the ministry of Christians that this book is directed. I hope that senior pastors, staff persons, and members of personnel committees will find it useful in their attempts to work together to fulfill the mission of the body.

Bill Carter
Johnson City, Tennessee

CONTENTS

1. The Apostolic Church Staff: New Testament
   Foundations for Local Church Ministry   9

2. The Edification of the Church: Building a
   Staff to Build the Body   27

3. Administering the Gifts: A New Perspective on
   Staff Management   53

4. Building the Team: The Foundations   74

5. Experiencing Spirituality: The Staff Growing
   Toward Its Core Ministry   106

6. Mediating Spirituality: The Core of Ministry   130

Postlude   157

Bibliography   159

CHAPTER ONE

The Apostolic Church Staff

New Testament Foundations for Local Church Ministry

The author of the Acts of the Apostles never imagined that we would be scouring the text for any clue we could find about the early church. There was no intention to provide a complete report of every activity. So it is a little surprising that we are able to discover a detailed account of the assembly of the first local church staff. It was like this:

After the incident of the Hellenistic widows reported in Acts 6 (a useful lesson in gender politics), there is a recognition that some people are better at preaching and praying and some are better at the "real work" of the church. Seven persons are chosen to do the distribution (perhaps as the first administrators?) while the apostles are freed up for serious witnessing. The whole scheme goes a little awry when some of the "deacons" prove to be better preachers than the evangelists, but the division is too advantageous for the apostles to abandon, so it continues to be practiced. Eventually most of the big shots tend to gather in Jerusalem while the local churches are left to fend for themselves.

Leadership did emerge to meet the challenge in most cases, but occasionally a situation came up that required a more direct involvement of the Jerusalem "cabinet."

The First Pastoral Appointment

Such a circumstance develops in Antioch, a metropolis at the northern end of the Mediterranean bulge. Normally the Jerusalem group keeps an eye on the spread of the faith, encouraging preaching, especially among Jewish congregations, and receiving regular reports from witnesses. But some unapproved evangelists from Cyprus and Cyrene begin making numerous Gentile converts in Antioch (Acts 11:19-20). When word gets back to Jerusalem, the decision is made to find a reliable person to pastor the new congregation, and so they make an "appointment" by sending Barnabas to the new charge.

✳Barnabas does well as a pastor. He makes everybody feel good and encourages them to grow in faith. In fact the congregation seems to declare that he is a "good man" (Acts 11:24), which probably meant the same about a pastor then as it does today: Everybody likes him, but he is no great shakes as a preacher or leader. However, he does have one admirable quality: He knows when he is in over his head. Upon realizing that he cannot handle the situation alone, he commences a search to find an assistant.

Whatever liabilities Barnabas may have, they do not include timidity. Since he needs help he decides to go for broke. He travels to Tarsus to find a person who has previously impressed him, although he certainly knows that the prospect is an outsider and is suspected of irregularities by many of the leaders of the church. The newcomer is Saul, later to be called Paul, who readily accepts the job.

The Apostolic Teacher

The first known staff member was not a clergyperson, or even a preacher, but a teacher. Paul is trained as a scholar, with a commitment to historical research and unusual skill at writing. Although he is known to be fiery and temperamental, with tendencies toward rebelliousness against authority (for evidence that he stayed that way, see Galatians 2), Barnabas feels that Saul can be a great help if properly supervised.

This estimate proves to be true. The two spend a whole year teaching in the church at Antioch (Acts 11:26), so successfully that the church becomes a center for the faith. The employment of the first Christian educator on a local church staff is a stroke of genius. In fact it is here that the believers are first called "Christians."

Paul never stops being a teacher and is known as an educator by his contemporaries. By the time of the writing of the letters to Timothy, he (or someone who wrote with knowledge of him) refers to himself as an "apostle and teacher" (1 Tim. 2:7; 2 Tim. 1:11). He always ranks teaching high on the lists of gifts of ministry and never claims to be an eloquent preacher. There are even times when he feels that he must defend himself against the charge that he is not an orator. His defense is that persons need to be taught at their own level of comprehension, and that great Christians are not made by great orators, but by persons who can communicate great truths in simple ways (1 Cor. 2:1-5).

While the new church has some troublesome tendencies, which eventually lead to a big confrontation between the two local leaders and the Jerusalem group (Acts 15), it rapidly develops ministries that are to be a model for the church for centuries. At one point it even provides the first assistance to a judicatory group (the apostles and elders in Jerusalem) when famine occurs. This assistance is delivered in person by Barnabas and Paul, and the elders send John Mark back to Antioch with them when they return (Acts 11:30; 12:25).

Multiple Staff Ministry

There are other persons on the staff at Antioch. Collectively they are called "prophets" and "teachers." Barnabas and Paul are part of the group, but there are others (note the plural in Acts 13). We can only guess at their roles, but it seems clear that a number of people are employed (with or without pay) in the total ministry of the local church, some with responsibilities related to proclamation and some as educators. (One of these is identified as "Simeon the black," so the staff is apparently interracial.) Since the ministry there seems to be in good hands, it is possible to respond to the guidance of the Holy Spirit and send the first "missionaries," Paul and Barnabas, into the field to preach and teach, leaving the other prophets and teachers to carry on the work at Antioch.

In the mission field the lessons learned about staff in the congregation at Antioch help set the pattern. The missionaries add John Mark to the retinue, as an assistant (or secretary). He may be a protégé of Peter, maybe even suggested by him for the job because of John Mark's loyalty to the organization. (John Mark later accompanied Peter on his travels.) However, he does not last long and his behavior becomes the subject of the first big staff quarrel.

Apparently Paul feels that John Mark has shirked his responsibilities when he leaves the group at Perga (in Pamphylia) to return to Jerusalem (Acts 13:13), but Barnabas wants to give John Mark a second chance. There is a hot argument and Barnabas departs taking John Mark with him. Silas, also from Jerusalem, becomes an assistant to Paul (15:40). That gives Paul the opportunity to bring in his own protégé to join Silas as a member of the team.

So, he goes to Galatia where he recruits Timothy, a young man with whom he had become acquainted on his visit there. Paul now has a staff that reflects his own understanding of the ministry and in whom he has complete confidence. That combination works well for a long period of time.

New Testament references to persons working alongside one another in ministry, both in the local church and in the mission field, are numerous. At the end of a number of his letters Paul refers to companions on the journey. And in Romans 16 (some persons think that passage was meant for Ephesus, but the principle is the same) he draws a list of fellow workers, some of whom (Prisca and Aquila, for instance) are known to have worked as "staff" in local churches. Others (Phoebe, Andronicus and Junia, Rufus, and so on) are obviously important figures in the spread of the good news. Wherever the faith went partnerships in ministry developed.

In the beginning Paul may not have had a fully developed doctrine of ministry and the church, but it is articulated in his letters to Corinth and Rome, and by the time of the Ephesian letter it becomes clear that the structure that held it all together is the concept of the gifts of ministry. We look briefly at that theme in order to gain a full understanding of the biblical foundation for the work of the Body of Christ, and its significance for staff function.

Learning What Christians Do

The earliest Christian community struggles to understand its task as a part of the plan of God for the redemption of persons. It plainly has a role (Jesus himself had said so), but it is not clear what this role is or how to define it in relationship to the spreading of the good news of the spiritual and moral victory represented by Jesus Christ. Nor is it obvious what kind of personnel is needed to accomplish the task once it is defined. It is a church looking for a way to meet its leadership needs.

Proclamation is an obvious factor. The word could not be heard without witnesses, and the community needed spokespersons to order its activities and guide its energies. The word "prophet" may be used to describe this proclamation role within the church, just as it had been used to describe spokespersons for God in the Old Testament. (See 1 Cor. 14:3.) This effort to proclaim the good news leads some persons in the community to the conclusion that preaching is all important. This assertion results in invidious divisions like that of Acts 6, in which some are set aside as servants of the body, leaving others free to give their time to "prayer and to serving the word" (Acts 6:4). That experiment in clergy and lay division produces some surprises (as already noted) because some of the deacons turn out to be better witnesses than some of the "apostles," but it does clearly establish that someone must do something besides proclamation if the community is to function well. So apostolic (or any other) preaching is not the whole task, and leaders cannot be defined in terms of speaking (witnessing) alone.

Healing ministries and the working of miracles intrigue many from the very beginning. Even during the life of Jesus some wonder how to produce these evidences in order to exhibit the power of God in themselves. A considerable number probably think that such demonstrations are so convincing that no other activity is needed to realize the goal of winning every person to the gospel and incorporating them into the church. However, this theory does not work well in practice. Not everyone can produce wondrous feats, and even when they do some observers are more dumbfounded than confirmed as believers. Again, something else is required for the faith community to be an effective agency for the gospel. Leaders cannot be defined only as those who can do miracles.

After Pentecost, and especially after the coming of the Holy Spirit to the Gentiles (Acts 13:44-48), there are apparently some who promote speaking in tongues as the chief evidence of the power of God among the disciples. It is suggested that such speaking is the principle proof of effectiveness among leaders. These persons (unknown, but possibly including Apollos) may have been scattered throughout the region but were certainly represented in the church at Corinth. It is persons from this church who caused Paul to address the meaning of Christian responsibility and the place of specific skills (gifts) in the life of the community. To understand staff function (and the function

of the church) it is very useful to reexamine Paul's reply to the
church at Corinth and subsequent developments in the definition of the Body of Christ and relationships between its parts.

The Gifts of Grace

The question from Corinth seems innocent enough. "Now
concerning spiritual gifts (*pneumatikos* is the transliteration from
the Greek, where *pneuma* means spirit), brothers and sisters, I
do not want you to be uninformed" (1 Cor. 12:1). A simple
statement, but one which implies that there is a considerable difference between the views of Paul and of those who champion
the "evidences of the spirit" as the standard of validity. It appears
that some in the early church are saying that one cannot prove
the possession of the Holy Spirit unless these *pneumatikos* are
present. Since the matter could be explosive for the church, Paul
speaks adroitly to the whole issue. Using the matter of spirituality as a starting point, he changes the focus of the entire discussion by using another word to describe the relationship of the
believer to the task of the church. He continues to talk about
spirituality but changes pointedly to the word *charismata* (hardly known outside the New Testament), which means something
like "marks of grace." In addition he deliberately relates the
whole matter to the whole of God, ending each phrase with one
of the parts of what we have come to call the Trinity: Spirit,
Lord, and God. "Now there are varieties of gifts, but the same
Spirit; and there are varieties of services, but the same *Lord;* and
there are varieties of activities, but it is the same *God* who acti-
vates all of them in everyone" (12:4-6 emphasis mine). Thereafter Paul will use this new term, *charismata,* almost exclusively
when referring to the gifts, as he often does.

From this point on it is his intention that the gifts will be
seen as the product of the whole Godhead, with the entire
trinitarian dynamic operating among the people of God. And
by using *charis* (grace) as the source, he identifies the gifts

with the process of justification: We are *justified* by grace, and *gifted* by grace. They are part of each other—complementary aspects of Christian experience. (In Ephesians 4:7 he writes that the *charismata* are given by Jesus Christ, another indication that he means more than just the Holy Spirit.)

Furthermore, he carefully names some of the gifts so that all will understand their variety and utility. In 1 Corinthians 12:8-10, he includes the expected items: prophecy (preaching), healing and miracle working, and speaking in tongues, but he adds wisdom, knowledge, faith, and discernment, all of which may relate to the process of teaching and learning. Later in verse 28, he enlarges the list to specifically mention teaching, helping (assistance), leadership, and administration. Most of these related to public leadership roles, so he made sure that more personal gifts were highlighted in his letter to Rome (12:3-8): encouragement (exhortation), giving, compassion (kindness). Both of these lists, and the one in Ephesians 4:11-16, end with the observation that no gift has meaning apart from love, which is the ultimate gift and the crowning glory of the Body of Christ.

By adding the environment of love to the exercise of the gifts, Paul has transformed them from mere capabilities to dynamic expressions of the fullness of spirituality. They are a continuation of the gift of God made on the cross, a part of the all-encompassing love which brought the faith into existence.

Of course the list is illustrative, not exhaustive. It will end only when all has been done that can ever be done for Christ. Items change as needs change. Some gifts are dramatic, others almost mundane. They may lie dormant until they are needed. Persons gifted by God for just such occasions emerge as leaders when the time is right. New gifts are planted in disciples for emerging needs. The whole process is so varied and energizing that it can never be understood from a single historical perspective. The Body of Christ, one body, is fueled and directed by a multitude of abilities (gifts/*charismata*), which are placed in a multitude of persons so that all are forced to work together, as a team, if any are to know the fullness of the church.

The Formation of the Body of Christ

The inquiry from Corinth has become the starting point for a description of the nature of the church, and the place of the individual Christian in it, which transformed the scattered, insecure community into a focused, energetic body. By redirecting the subject from "how to prove that you have the Holy Spirit," to "how to find your place in the plan of God," Paul has discovered how the power of God can bring meaning from even the most potentially divisive situations.

The change from *pneuma*/spirit to *charis*/grace brings three important ideas to the forefront of the Christian doctrine of the church as the Body of Christ:

1. The gifts originate in the same place as salvation. We are saved by grace, and gifted by grace. God has done both in order to achieve his ultimate purpose. This relationship is made very clear in Ephesians 2:8-10: "For by grace you have been saved through faith, and this is not your own doing; it is the gift of God—not the result of works, so that no one may boast. *For we are what he has made us, created in Christ Jesus for good works, which God prepared beforehand* to be our way of life" (emphasis mine). The works of the law, which are useless, are supplanted by the good works of grace, to be done by gifted persons in a design of God's own choosing, which turns out to involve the church.

2. The gifts are the building blocks of the church, hereafter often called the Body of Christ. In 1 Corinthians 12:7, Paul says, "To each is given the manifestation of the Spirit for the common good." Later, in Ephesians 4:11-12, the point is made even more crisply: "The gifts he gave were . . . to equip the saints for the work of ministry, for building up the body of Christ." In the latter part of verse 16 the concept is completed with the claim that, "as each part is working properly, [it] promotes the body's growth in building itself up in love."

The church is the sum of its members' gifts, which were given to each by God in order that the whole task might be accomplished.

3. The gifts are not to be distinguished in value, since all are equally necessary and therefore equally important, whether the community or the individual realizes it or not. Furthermore, the variety of the gifts is essential: *If all were gifted in the same way there would not be a body,* but a single organ which could not function alone (1 Cor. 12:14-31). The Body of Christ celebrates the variety of the gifts and recognizes that being different is part of the plan of God. In the letter to the church at Rome Paul is again explicit: "For as in one body we have many members, and not all the members have the same function, so we, who are many, are one body in Christ, and individually we are members one of another" (Rom. 12:4-5). And, of course, all are tied together by love, the indispensable ingredient of the life together in Christ.

Just as the revelation of the process of salvation in the letter to the Galatians resulted in the insight that "there is no longer Jew or Greek, there is no longer slave or free, there is no longer male and female; for all of you are one in Christ Jesus" (Gal. 3:28), so the revelation that the gifts make up the church leads to the inescapable conclusion that since God has arranged for everyone to have a place according to his purpose (1 Cor. 12:18), then each participant in the plan is equally important. Even "the members of the body that seem to be weaker are indispensable" (12:22). *Ministry is the function of the whole body in which each member has an irreplaceable role.*

Body Language

The language of the Body of Christ is ministry, and the parts of speech are the gifts (abilities). The rules of its grammar are those which derive from the principle of love, and all of the actions of the body must be consistent with the personal and spiritual plan of the one who brought it into being and is now its head, Jesus Christ. It is one ministry with many facets (not a collection of separate ministries) and may not be divided into differentiated segments. Since each of its expressions is necessary for the whole to exist, then the various dialects (denominations) and accents (theological perspectives) do not constitute separate forms of speech, only differing aspects of communication for the total body. Any competition between classes (clergy, elders, lay, diaconal, teams, and so on) or groups (sexes, races, denominations) is inappropriate, because each is doing a task that contributes to the fulfillment of the whole ministry of God.

In the light of this understanding of the body, its gifts, and its ministry, there are certain conclusions we can reach about the place and function of volunteer and paid ministers within the body. These observations, drawn from the story of the first staffs and the theme of the gifts of ministry, may be arranged to form a body of standards for staff and congregational ministry.

Some Basic Principles

1. *Staff recruitment and development should be in response to the mission of the body.* Until Antioch it seems perfectly adequate to have a corps of itinerant preachers who proclaim the message of salvation. This new body, however, requires a different approach. Its people, being drawn from a Gentile background, are ignorant of Old Testament tradition, have no knowledge of the workings of faith, and need both pastoral care and information. Prophets and teachers are in order. It works.

Subsequently the church needs to reach out, so a missionary staff is created. Still later congregations need organization, so deacons and elders and like offices are put in place. At every stage persons are arranged to do ministry in the most effective way. Staff development is a product of mission. Changing mission means changing staff, sometimes through new positions and persons, sometimes through new roles for those already at work.

2. *Faith and a willingness to grow in its practice are a necessity for all who work in the body.* Barnabas seems never to waver, while Paul changes every day, yet each shows a determination to pursue

a more mature spirituality. Both show an attachment to the core of faith. Paul later decries those who "fell in love with the present world" and deserted the mission, affirming that personal faith is a necessary component of effective ministry. Skills are not enough by themselves. They must be applied within a deep connection into the ground of the faith, into the teaching of the apostles.

3. *Persons chosen for staff positions must possess and be able to exhibit gifts of ministry consistent with the mission of the body.* Each person has different gifts, and some have many, but the particular ability needed for the realization of mission in a specific body must be present in some way. Persons need to feel called and gifted to do what they are invited to do. The most impressive recruit can be the biggest disappointment if gifts do not coincide with mission. The person who brings irrelevant gifts, however brilliant, can be a serious detriment, because there is the danger that we will accommodate the mission to the gifts instead of the proper sequence of gifts to mission.

In one community a congregation had employed a brilliant organist. His knowledge of music and skill at the console were legendary. He would allow only classically appropriate music in weddings and the "great" hymns on Sundays. Finally he concluded that the pipe organ in the church was inadequate for his level of artistry and enlisted some parishioners in a crusade to redo the sanctuary acoustics and buy the best organ available.

There was resistance to the project. Some felt that the best organ is a mark of a great church, some that it is an ego satisfaction for the organist. Although the project won a close vote of the board, and was completed, the church was hopelessly split. Many people left, including a majority of the supporters of the organ project. The organ, perhaps unjustly, became a continuing symbol of the triumph of vanity over ministry for those who remained.

All gifts must be appropriate to the setting. Paul, the scholar, is a perfect addition to the staff at Antioch, but might have been a pain in the neck at the Jerusalem headquarters (as some of us are reputed to be in our own denominational settings). There is a place for everyone in some ministry, somewhere. But no one can contribute to every ministry exactly what it needs to accomplish its mission.

4. *Competence in the gifts of ministry is more important than conformity with traditional norms.* While a certain level of professional preparation and a commitment to the broader community are expected and even necessary, the staff person is first a participant in the mission of the local body and his or her gifts in the area of assigned ministry are of primary value. Background, theological orientation, and personal style may be factors in compatibility, which will be mentioned later, but competence and interpersonal skills are of the first order. Paul could not be considered one of the "good old boys," but he was very good at what he did. Some may have some skills, but not all those needed. Where some skills are absent it is important to provide training (as with Barnabas, who taught alongside Paul to encourage skill development) to ensure that the job gets done. Competence is the foundation for the practice of the gifts.

5. *Good interpersonal relationships are vital to effective performance and to spiritual growth.* Even the most dedicated and best trained persons may not work well together. When staff performance is deterred by incompatibilities of personality or values, it is necessary to find ways of realigning persons and relationships for more effective ministry. That may take the form of developing effective interpersonal relationships through a process of group spiritual search, training in interpersonal dynamics, using conflict resolution, or some other process of change and adaptation. When none of these work it is in the interest of mission to separate or regroup, as did Paul, Barnabas, and John Mark. John Mark seems to have been as great an asset to Peter as he never could be to Paul (1 Pet. 5:13). Barnabas is free to continue his

ministry of encouragement and affection, while Paul and his co-workers thrive in the mission to the far corners of the empire.

✦6. *Members of a church staff should work together, alongside one another, in the performance of ministry.* As Paul and Barnabas work together at the teaching task in Antioch, so must persons at all times work side by side, sharing the ministry, helping one another, teaching one another, and completing the mission of the body by becoming complete in the expression of the whole ministry of the people of God, whose foundation is *love,* an indispensable underpinning to the gifts of ministry (1 Corinthians 13). It has become fashionable to call this process "teamwork," but it might also be called "vocational maturity"—the harmony of the called.

7. *The Body of Christ is constructed of the gifts of its members and nothing else can replace these building blocks.* Employed and "volunteer" leaders, as well as the membership of the local Body of Christ, are gifted in ways that can help build the body. Every effort should be made to bring all of these gifts to prominence at appropriate times. However, none of us has the authority to use the power of office, influence, or denominational polity to structure the body or direct its activities in ways that deny or manipulate the gifts (Eph. 4:13-16).

8. *The basic task of the designated leadership is to discover the gifts of the members of the body and provide them arenas for expression.* While it is always appropriate to seek and use the gifts of persons in the perceived mission of a particular body, it is even more important to discern the gifts in order to *find* the mission of the body. The presence of gifted persons is itself a clue to the nature of the mission of the congregation, for if God has placed certain gifts within the body it may have been God's plan that these be employed in the total ministry of the body. It is not sufficient for the designated leadership to find persons to carry out only their vision of the ministry; they must also discover what mission or missions are implied by the nature of the gifts of the members.

9. *The ministry of any body (congregation) is a continuous*

*expression of the will of God, and each part has equal value with all
the others: paid or volunteer, ordained or unordained.* There is not
a separate ministry for laypersons or those who are "ordained"
or "consecrated." Nor is one of these groups more important to
the whole than the others. Although they may have different
responsibilities within a particular group or setting, they cannot
function without one another and are therefore completely
interdependent. All work alongside one another.

10. *Ministry is always an expression of the particular gifts of
the individual within the general context of the mission of the
body.* (A) All persons must be encouraged to find and employ
their gifts, and (B) each must be prepared to give way to others whose gifts may be more appropriate in any given setting.
The nature of the gifts will determine where the individual best
fits within the stream of ministry flowing from the body. *It is
not appropriate to make decisions on leadership or assignments of
responsibility on the basis of rank or position.* The only way to
engage persons in suitable tasks is to employ them in ways that
best express their gifts in the realization of the mission of the
body, whatever their position in the hierarchies of the church.

Richard J. Foster has a provocative word to say about the
nature of authority:

> Jesus never taught that everyone had equal authority. In fact, he
> had a great deal to say about genuine spiritual authority and taught
> that many did not possess it. But the authority of which Jesus
> spoke was not the authority of the pecking order. We must clearly
> understand the radical nature of Jesus' teaching on this matter. He
> was not revising the pecking order, he was abolishing it. The
> authority of which he spoke was not an authority of manipulation
> and control. It was an authority of function, not status.
> (*Celebration of Discipline* [San Francisco: Harper, 1988], p. 127)

In other words, the functions, which flow out of the gifts, are
the heart of the matter.

Each one is at the mercy of his or her own gifts and the

grace of God. These are the only resources that any minister
has to offer the body, and the only ones that will build up the
church. As Paul points out in 1 Corinthians 12:22-26, we all
suffer when one of us fails and rejoice when one of us succeeds. We are each called to apply the balm of the gifts to the
healing and strengthening of the body, or of life itself. To
claim or assume more is to replace the unity of the body with
the arrogance of individual ambition, which is the worst sin
against both the church and God, as explained by Paul in
Romans 12: "I say to everyone among you not to think of
yourself more highly than you ought to think, but to think
with sober judgment. . . . For as in one body we have many
members, and not all the members have the same function,
so we, who are many, are one body in Christ, and individually we are members one of another" (vv. 3-5).

We all are in this together and cannot exclude one another
without diminishing the power of the body.

An Exercise on the Gifts

Here is a simple way of helping persons reflect on the gifts.
It may assist the staff in reviewing and discussing the gifts.

A) Give the checklist to each staff person.

B) After everyone has completed the form, ask for a volun-
    teer to name an item he or she has checked. Whatever it
    is affirm its value, and then ask how many others marked
    that same item. Repeat the question, and procedure, five
    or six times or until everyone has had time to respond.

C) Ask the group what conclusions they draw from the
    items persons marked. (They will often say things like
    "Not everybody claims the same abilities," or, "There is a
    wide variety of abilities in our group," or, "We need each
    of these abilities at some time.") Make a list of comments
    on chalkboard or newsprint.

A New Way of Looking at the Gifts

Check 2 to 4 of the following that you feel you are good at.

_____ 1. Explaining things to people

_____ 2. Telling others about the faith

_____ 3. Tending to people's needs

_____ 4. Helping persons understand each other

_____ 5. Communicating in dramatic ways

_____ 6. Taking charge when needed

_____ 7. Understanding the meaning of things

_____ 8. Making people feel cared for

_____ 9. Giving graciously

_____10. Speaking before groups

_____11. Making unusual things happen

_____12. Identifying religious frauds

_____13. Encouraging and supporting others

_____14. Gathering and using information

_____15. Listening or acting sympathetically

_____16. Helping people toward health

_____17. Maintaining calm in times of stress

_____18. Arranging meetings and programs.

Team Spirituality: A Guide for Staff and Church by William J. Carter. Copyright ©
1997 by Abingdon Press. Reprinted by permission.

D) Identify the abilities listed in A using only these words or
   phrases:

1. Teaching	11. Miracles
2. Witnessing/evangelizing	12. Recognition of true
3. Serving/helping	and false spirits
4. Interpretation	13. Encouragement
5. Tongues	14. Knowledge
6. Leadership (authority)	15. Kindness
7. Wisdom/understanding	16. Healing
8. Pastoring	17. Faith
9. Giving	18. Administration
10. Preaching/prophecy	

Point out that this way of stating the meaning of the gifts
mentioned in the New Testament is intended to show that
they are generally not mysterious or exotic but normal qualities of human beings that God can use. Also stress that these
are only illustrative, not exhaustive. There are hundreds of
gifts. Paul mentioned new ones each time he wrote about
them (1 Corinthians 12–14; Romans 12; Ephesians 4). If he
had lived longer he might have added scores to the list. All
are of God and all are useful. Ask if persons can name other
gifts not in this list.

E) Close by forming a circle. Ask the staff members to volunteer
   what gift each feels he or she brings to the group. Ask the
   group to respond with, "Thank you, Lord," after each item.
   When all have had a chance to contribute, close with prayer.

This is the first of a number of instruments and interactive
exercises that you will be offered throughout the book. You
may have your own, or some brought back from workshops
and seminars that seem more useful to you in making the
point. By all means use them. The staff will grow as it inter-
acts, and the learning process should be encouraged in every
way possible.

CHAPTER TWO

The Edification of the Church

Building a Staff to Build the Body

Most of us think that "staff" implies a number of persons working together, each of whom has a well-defined role. We imagine that the ideal staff is one in which each person is semi-autonomous with only occasional need for coordination and calendaring by a director, who also checks for efficiency and effectiveness. While this model may actually exist in the business world, and in a few churches, it is far more common to find a church staff composed of persons with multiple responsibilities and constantly changing roles. Each staff is unique. There are no ideal structures or job descriptions because there are no generic congregations. Each is a fully functioning part of the Body of Christ and each has its own mission to pursue and its own ministry to perform at each stage in its development.

If the church is a body, its staff are limbs and organs. The ministry of the staff flows out of the ministry of the local church—which flows out of the presence of Christ in the body. As the church perceives its own mission and ministry and begins to embody it in congregational and community life, it may realize that some tasks are beyond the time, skills, and energy of its members and its pastor. Where financial resources are available the church may then seek to employ persons for those areas in which it feels a lack of effectiveness. And so—a staff is born, not so much out of a spiritually rational process as from a desire to eliminate deficiencies, which may seem to be a very commendable goal. The only difficulty is that staff persons hired to remedy "deficiencies" rather than fulfill goals are likely to be judged by standards which come out of frustration and blame rather than those developed as an expression of the whole mission of the church.

The employment of the very first staff member, and every one thereafter, should be the product of a careful and prayerful examination of the mission and ministry of the local church for that moment in history and the place of the gifts of each member and staff person in the fulfillment of that mission. Which means that the first step in the development of a staff position is to examine the church's mission and goals. Although this is not the place for a discourse on mission statements, it is an appropriate opportunity to review their merits. Many churches have not thought a mission discovery process was necessary because they feel that "everybody already knows" or that "the Bible tells us what our purpose is." Such declarations have marginal validity, but if we are the Body of Christ and the gifts of ministry are our chief resource, then every person and every group has a unique place in the total plan of God. Seeking to understand our mission is not only a legitimate activity but a necessary one for all churches, and, indeed, for all agencies of the church. Here is a sample statement:

Statement of Mission

Glorifying God Through Knowing Christ and Making Him Known

Freed by the risen Christ and blessed by the Holy Spirit, we, as a fellowship of believers, will strive to glorify God through:

Winning Others to Christ

"Go therefore and make disciples of all nations, baptizing them in the name of the Father and of the Son and of the Holy Spirit." (Matt. 28:19)

Serving Others

"Do not use your freedom as an opportunity for self-indulgence, but through love become slaves to one another." (Gal. 5:13)

Growing Spiritually

"But grow in the grace and knowledge of our Lord and Savior Jesus Christ." (2 Pet. 3:18)

Nurturing Members

"And let us consider how to provoke one another to love and good deeds, not neglecting to meet together . . . but encouraging one another." (Heb. 10:24-25)

Leading and Serving the Church Community

"Let your light shine before others, so that they may see your good works and give glory to your Father in heaven." (Matt. 5:16)

The mission statement of a congregation is the product of an examination of the gifts, vision, and circumstances of the membership in the light of its understanding of Scripture, its denominational history, and its perception of the needs of its community and world. Each mission is different because the gifts of the members and the physical and spiritual dynamics of each body are different.

The mission of the local church is unique. It may be similar to what other churches see as their mission, but it is fundamentally different. Programs or organizational methodologies from other "successful" churches may be helpful, but only as a tool after the church has succeeded in identifying its own unique place. While denominational history is a part of the identity of the body, and is part of the call of God to that congregation, current denominational emphases or programs cannot be substituted for the examination of God's will for this body in this time and place. Nothing can replace the immersion of the congregation in the search for the will of God for these people at this point in history.

The way the church perceives its mission will determine its organizational mode, its methods, and many of its activities. The number and job descriptions of staff are intimately related to how the church understands its part in the whole Body of Christ. The gifts, tasks, and roles of staff persons must be consistent with the mission of the church. When the mission changes the roles of staff need to be reexamined. A staff person or an entire staff chosen in any other context is likely to be ultimately unappreciated and ineffective.

Starting Up: Choosing the First Staff Member

We tend to think of staff as the prerogative of the large church. Actually churches of many sizes have staff persons, from the church with an average attendance of 100 that employs only a single part-time person in addition to the pastor, to the megachurch with a crew of dozens. This section, and the entire book, intends to address that whole spectrum.

It is a rare experience to participate in describing the kind of person needed and choosing the very first staff person in a congregation. Most churches take that step with hardly a thought, assuming that the first person hired ought to be a "secretary" who will do the routine tasks of the church office to free the pastor for more "spiritual" involvements. (Remember the division of labor in the sixth chapter of Acts?) In some cases that turns out to be just right. In some it may be a terrible mistake. Changes in the church's role in the community, in its methods of operation, and especially in the proliferation of technology (word processors, copying machines, telephone answering services, etc.) have opened other means of handling information.

For instance, one church decided to have its bulletin and letters prepared by a church member who knew how to operate a word processor, hiring this "community visitor" as the first staff person. Area growth and the urgency of reaching new residents were most important.

A newly established church felt called to create lay-led cells as its primary organization for spiritual growth and recruited only a basic office-communications technical person and a corps of part-time trainers to equip its cell leaders.

Another church, with a strong commitment to helping those in need in the community, hired a person to manage the distribution of funds, oversee the used clothing center, and monitor services for the needy (the Acts 6 experience, again!), as well as answer the church telephone and do minor typing and copying.

One older small-town church had a large facility used by many community groups and decided that it needed a facilities manager who could also do some program development, leaving the paperwork to a pastor who was gifted with typing proficiency and had a keen interest in computers. The time saved from taking care of the building more than made up for the few hours the pastor now spent at the routine communications.

In each case the employment of a staff person responded to a felt need of the church, and, just as important, the principle of the gifts was made explicit: The work of the church should proceed from the gifts instead of from hierarchical models. We shouldn't hire a "secretary" to do the office work, and then create office work to take up the time of the secretary. We shouldn't make the work fit the position; instead, we need to utilize the gifts of persons in ways that make them feel they are in ministry.

Of course there are times when what we need is indeed a person to do the office work—and fortunately there are persons who feel the call to manage the office in a way that adds to the ministry of the church. In such cases the most important thing we can do is to find a way to describe the job, and title it, so as to make it clear that this person is a minister, too, called to be a part of the mission of the congregation. More than once I have received a call from a pastor planning to bring the staff to a workshop who asked whether the secretary ought to be included. The answer is always the same—everyone who is employed by the church to do any aspect of its ministry is a member of the staff, and all should be involved in any growth opportunities that may be available.

Building a Staff

Each person added to the staff should be recruited with the same care as the first. The purpose of building the staff is to build the body by adding new gifts to the total (Eph. 4:12-16). A staff is built to accommodate growth, changed directions, newly perceived needs, or to provide additional spiritual resources. The process of building should include:

1. A continuous reassessment of the church and its ministry, with the participation of the congregation.

2. Constant involvement of the staff in defining and evaluating its relation to the body and its tasks.

3. The development of descriptions of needed functions by appropriate committees or councils, and the assessment of the availability of financial resources.

4. The search for persons with gifts and skills to fulfill those functions, within and beyond the community, full-time or part-time.

Positions, titles, and roles are not fixed. They are a product of the stages of growth and may need to be reordered as the perception of ministry evolves. Beginning with a pastor, an office assistant, part-time music and maintenance persons, the congregation might add a part-time age-level director and a volunteer facilities manager. A little later there could be an associate pastor/youth director, a clerical/facilities person, a director of program (or, if preferred, a director of spiritual growth), and a music director/organist. A next stage might involve a full-time secretary, a financial manager/facilities administrator, an associate in spiritual formation (ordained or lay), another in congregational development (to assimilate members, etc.), a music director and an organist, with part-time persons for youth ministry and for older-adult ministry, with the building cared for by a cleaning service—or any other sequence that fits the mission of the church and the gifts of the available personnel.

If persons with these gifts cannot be found it may be necessary to redefine the jobs.

5. A constant openness to the possibility that gifted persons may emerge from the congregation. God may be leading through the presence of these gifted persons. Some of the most effective staff may be those who have felt the call of God within the congregational vision. They may help point the way to mission.

6. The incorporation of these persons into the life of the staff and the church. Staff persons cannot merely be technicians. Nor can part-time be interpreted to mean peripheral. They are body parts—integral to the life and ministry of the congregation. They are the bearers of ministry: of the ministry of the congregation, but more significantly, of the ministry of Jesus Christ. They are participants in the completion of the whole ministry of God in this setting.

Where Do We Find Staff Persons?

Just a few years ago the recruitment of staff usually began within an academic qualifications matrix. Professionalism was stressed, and graduates of seminaries, schools of Christian education, and college music majors were eagerly sought. As the number of churches employing staff has grown some changes have occurred:

❑ The supply of clergy with specialized skills has decreased.
❑ There are fewer schools of Christian education.
❑ Congregation staff job descriptions have changed focus.
❑ In some cases there has even been a reaction to "professionalism" on the grounds that it decreases the ability of the staff person to relate well to the needs and perspectives of his or her constituencies.

In addition, two important shifts are occurring throughout the church:

1) The churches are beginning to perceive themselves as reservoirs of gifted persons who may themselves be able to do the ministry the body needs to respond to the call of God, and

2) ministry is moving more and more into the community instead of taking place entirely within the facilities and program environment of the congregation.

Once a direction has been selected by the governing board or council of the congregation (often through the leadership of the pastor and the staff team), the recruitment of persons to complete the vision begins. The staff already in place may be able to adjust to the new vision, but there may be need for adding or changing staff positions and responsibilities. (The stronger the vision and the wider the paradigm shift the more likely it is that big changes in training, functions, relationships, and personnel will be necessary.)

There is an accelerating trend to draw staff persons from within the congregation or community. There are a number of good reasons for that redirection: (1) Those who are part of the body that claimed the vision and set the mission are more likely to be sympathetic to its goals and committed to the discipline necessary for their fulfillment. (2) There are fewer potential staff persons available from traditional sources, and those who are may not be prepared for innovative ministries by their prior training or experience. (3) Since the expression of the gifts is an important ingredient of all ministry, choosing persons within the community of faith enables more gifts to be employed. And (4) when persons live within the community there is much more flexibility in deployment of personnel. It is very difficult to ask someone to move into the community for a part-time position, or to require the family of a talented person to move from friends, employment, or established residence in another community in order for the church to have the personnel it needs. Efficient recruitment requires the use of all options, and promising options exist within the body. (For a more detailed view of this option see Brian K. Bauknight, *Body Building* [Nashville: Abingdon Press, 1996].)

One word of caution. The use of either part-time or local persons to avoid paying "benefits" as a way of reducing the cost of staff has serious ethical problems. The church or its pastor should not become party to any scheme that deprives gifted workers of basic levels of support in order to save money for some other project. Gifts administration is never less than fully loving and caring in all areas of staff support. We should love our staff members as ourselves.

However, making use of the traditional sources—seminaries, schools of Christian education, technical schools, and other academic environments—is still feasible. Many such institutions are in the forefront of training for ministries and can and will provide recommendations of persons with special skills. One of the advantages of these sources is that trained but inexperienced persons may be much more amenable to innovation than those with long experience. Sometimes familiarity breeds contempt—for change.

With appropriate ethical safeguards it is possible to recruit staff persons from other churches or church agencies. There are persons out there who have completed their ministries in one site and are waiting for an opportunity to answer the call of God in a new ministry field. Often the employing church recognizes the readiness for a move and will be very supportive, realizing that they need personnel for a new direction, or for a fresh start. Such persons may have many of the skills and experiences needed to develop a new ministry area in the church to which they are being called.

Excellent staff persons are often available from other occupational or professional arenas, such as school teaching, business management, service occupations, public relations, marketing, or health services. Sometimes specific skills will be of great assistance, but more often it is the underlying ability or personality that transfers to the church environment. Second-career persons are becoming more numerous, both as ordained and unordained workers. Even dual careers are not uncommon, serving in one occupation and devoting some quality time to another. As individuals become aware that callings occur at any stage of life and listen for the voice of God, they sometimes become prime candidates for church staffs.

Identifying Basic Staff Positions

There are always questions about which staff positions are indispensable. What does constitute a basic staff—especially in the light of the present movement toward greater lay membership involvement, both paid and volunteer, and the growth of cell-based structures for congregational ministries? Of course the answer to that will differ in relation to the size and location of the building and the community, but for churches large and small there are some ministry positions that will probably be around for the next few decades. Where needs and resources coalesce these functions will be needed in most churches, in full-time or part-time positions, and some training or experience is helpful. That will mean that professional or semiprofessional personnel will continue to have a place, even though it is clear that the trend is toward more and more use of persons from within the body itself. Some of these positions are:

❏ pastor (even that is questioned by some), music leaders
❏ communications (secretaries), age level specialists
❏ business manager (financial officer), maintenance persons
❏ congregational care and outreach ministries
❏ director of program or lay ministries (or both)

What about the future? What staff positions seldom filled today might become common as part-time or full-time in the twenty-first century?

Director of Marketing is one. With the increasing competition for the attention of the public we may have to use more of the methods of public relations to attract prospects.

Coordinator of Spiritual Growth. Some churches are already designating staff in that field. Others may follow.

Dean of the Lay Pastor's School. The need for more and more persons trained in the caring skills and small-group leadership could well justify the use of paid or volunteer persons to do training, with a dean to oversee the curriculum and process.

Administrator of Community Ministries could be another designation. Outreach into the area around the church with appropriate responses to community needs may call some persons.

Make your own list. Needs for staff change constantly. The church must change with the needs. Strong growth or a shift to a seven-day a week programming mode might mean more and different staff positions. A successful lay ministries program or structuring the church around small groups instead of program units could mean the involvement of so many more laity in leadership roles that fewer staff would be needed. The need to support special ministries might require the channeling of funds to missions instead of local staff. Ministry outreach could occupy some staff who would be paid by the congregation but set apart for services in another community, city, or country. (Remember the church at Antioch sending Paul and Barnabas?) The body is a dynamic entity and requires constant adjustment, including staff, to achieve its mission.

It should be noted that none of these positions requires ordination, or precludes it. Lay pastors often work in small churches and newly planted congregations, and they could well do the work of larger parishes if needed and properly equipped. Pastoring is a calling, a role, a gift, not necessarily a designated order. In the same way, ordained persons can do any of the tasks mentioned here, and others, when called and equipped. There are no artificial barriers to effective staff work within the gifts environment.

It is also very clear that both men and women are eligible for all roles. Male secretaries and female pastors are becoming more numerous, and we are discovering that the old myopia that caused us to see New Testament leadership as reserved for males only was simply a mistake. When Paul wrote in Galatians 3:28, after revealing that grace through faith was the source of justification, "There is no longer Jew or Greek, there is no longer slave or free, there is no longer male and female; for all of you are one in Christ Jesus," he really meant it—and he was speaking for God. Both women and men are appropriate for all staff roles.

With the change to more and more part-time local persons as staff there is also the danger that male presence in staffs will become more rare. Recently, to my seminars a number of churches have brought staffs with no male except the pastor. There are complex reasons for men dropping out of church, but it would be as tragic to give the impression that staff roles are only for women as it was to imply that they were only for men.

The employment of staff is a product of the church's view of its mission, and its understanding of the gifts of its members. Staff should be chosen to supplement the work of the membership rather than replace it. There is definitely a place for paid staff, but only after the congregation has defined what it is called to do, and what its members and pastor cannot do.

Orientation and Training for New Staff

Wherever they come from, staff persons will need orientation and training for their new roles. It cannot be assumed that even the most experienced will have the information or specific skills for their new tasks, and every staff job is a new one, in a new church, with a new administrator. More misunderstanding occurs during the definition and entry stage of employment than at any other time. The effects often last throughout the tenure of the staff person. Staff administrators should set up preventive training models.

A) Some process should be initiated to familiarize the new staff person with the church and community. They need some history, a list of the current goals, an overview of the structure and the groups in ministry (along with a judicious identification of relevant influential leaders), a discussion of values and customs, and any other reality-based, observable characteristics. Almost anyone can do this: the pastor, the chair of the pastor/staff committee, the chair of the board, or any experienced layperson. Just be sure that the one who does the orienting (including the pastor) has the capacity for objectivity!

B) Since many staff persons may be from other denominations or "independent" congregations, or unfamiliar with their own, there should be a place for an introduction to the heritage and current directions of any larger body of which the local one is a part. It is in vogue during these days of institution-bashing for persons to downgrade denominational affiliation, but there is more to be said about that—denominational emphases may be part of God's plan, too. If persons are gifted, why not institutions that were created from out of the gifts? In any case, a vast majority of churches with staffs still belong to and value some identifiable body, so any new staff persons should know enough to relate well to the rest of the organization, especially if the pastor and church expect to continue some or all of the traditional values. The pastor, a well-versed member of the congregation, or a course in doctrine and polity from a nearby denominational college or seminary would all be possibilities.

C) As a separate or extended part of the training in congregational or denominational emphases, every staff person should be made familiar with the scriptural basis of the ministry (local or extended) to which the body feels that it is called. It is good to remind ourselves once in a while that there are more than 1,000 denominations (and every time an "independent" church is formed there is another one), and every one of them firmly believes that its origin is based on Scripture. That may mean a particular interpretation of some portion of Scripture, or an emphasis on some scriptures rather than others, or even some belief *about* the Scripture rather than something based upon it. In any case persons who are to do the work of the church need to be acquainted with the scriptural foundation of their ministry. That serves two purposes: (1) It reassures persons in ministry that they do not need to fear attacks from those with a different interpretation or emphasis (I preached a series of sermons once on the topic "It's our Bible, TOO," which proved to be very popular), and (2) it allows them to decide whether they can support the scripture and the ministry. If they cannot they probably would do better elsewhere.

D) It is necessary for the new staff person to be familiar with the way the staff is currently structured (if it is) and any specific practices and expectations related to staff life. One way of accomplishing this step might be to devote a staff meeting to letting the staff share with the new person their perceptions about how things work and how to stay out of trouble (if that is possible). It could be that participation by a silent pastor in such a session might reveal some things he or she did not already know.

The process of orientation assures persons that we take them seriously. It communicates our concern for their comfort, and implies that we want them around for the long run, and in the whole ministry of the body.

Becoming Parts of the Body

The most important step beyond the first may be the last—the incorporation of persons. New and revised staff roles are at the mercy of the staff administrator (usually, but not always, the pastor) and personnel committees. When they are made to feel welcome in the staff, recognized and given stature in the congregation, appropriately evaluated and advised, and involved in the total life of the community of faith, they will function at a much higher level than if they are ignored, made an object of public scrutiny, or forced to "prove themselves" by uninformed judgments on their skills or personalities. Only the most unusual person can make the grade without the help of those who are responsible for the maintenance of staff image and morale. It is a vital function of the body to accept and nurture its members, converting them into *body parts,* members of one another—staff or otherwise.

William Schutz in his seminars on interpersonal relationships offers a simple outline of group dynamics which may be helpful in visualizing the process of incorporation within the staff or the church:

Phase 1—INCLUSION. The first need of persons in groups is acceptance. Commitment is really a product of the feeling of inclusion. Those who feel that their presence is important to others will be there, and be working. The ultimate product is trust. Schutz reminds us that nothing else of importance will take place in a work group until the inclusion phase has been completed satisfactorily. It is hoped that it will occur naturally as persons are brought into relationship with one another, but structured inclusion processes should be used if necessary.

Phase 2—CONTROL. Within a short time the group reaches a stage in which decisions must be made about matters of control: who is going to be in charge. Most of the time concerns about control issues come from a genuine desire to do things better. Sometimes, especially if the inclusion phase has not worked well or is incomplete, competitiveness or hostility may be exhibited. Openly or covertly there are contests for leadership. An "anti-leader" may emerge, who then becomes the resident critic of the senior pastor or others in positions of authority. Control issues may become roadblocks. Unless the resulting distrust and animosity can be resolved the effectiveness of the staff may suffer. The general rule for groups that get stuck in this phase is that reinitiating inclusion may help more than anything else. More time spent in getting to know one another, more examination of relationships, and more interactive decision making may help to get beyond the resistance. With pastoral assistance, and, if necessary, the use of persons with expertise in conflict resolution, these steps may yet build a successful working relationship.

Phase 3—AFFECTION. Affection is the driver of group life. (Even though Schutz is a consultant to business rather than churches, he has identified a basic Christian theme, love, as the center of all group life.) It is what everyone would like to gain, and what will make the group whole. It is so important that if the entire group cannot find a satisfactory level of affection some will separate and become affectionate with one another, creating cliques and rival social groups. But affection often happens. When it does there is stability, sharing, and support. Persons trust one another and cooperate in mutual projects and activities. It can be one of the most satisfying experiences ever.

But even this phase has its pitfalls. It is possible for the group to grow so affectionate that it becomes complacent, or even isolationist, holding itself apart from those outside, even from its own constituencies. Many small churches proudly proclaim how much their members love one another, but they are unable to extend that affection to newcomers. Church staffs can be like that, too.

Phase 4—MISSION. In addition to those named by Schutz, I have added this phase as a result of comments in early seminars. For church staffs there may be a phase in which there is a strong focus on the vision or tasks and a common endeavor to reach goals set by the group. It goes beyond affection in the sense that it replaces interpersonal satisfaction with the joy of interacting with the will of God.

But it too can be misdirected. A life consumed with high purpose may become separated from its roots in love. Some of the hardest workers are the least forgiving. Some of the most seemingly "spiritual" people are the ones who miss the mark of love the most. As we do with the other phases, we must put mission in the context of the whole of life and judge it by the gospel standards of love for God and persons: spirituality and affection. The primary administrative advice offered by Schutz is that the sensitive leader tries to discern where the group is and move them on toward the next phase. He or she assists inclusion, sorts out control, and affirms and participates in affection, making sure that the group moves beyond self-centered affection to a wider purpose, and then becomes inclusive once more as it takes more persons into the circle. It is this movement which defines the task of incorporation. At each turn of the cycle the possibility for deeper unity and more effective action grows. (Some of this material can be found in Schutz, *Joy* [New York: Grove Press, 1967].)

An Exercise in Group Process

In some workshops I have asked staffs to evaluate themselves in terms of where they feel they are in this cycle, by using the I.C.A.M. wheel, based on the Schutz typology of groups. Each is asked to put a checkmark beside the number which best describes where he or she feels the staff now is. Then the numbers are shared with the whole staff and they discuss (1) how they are alike, (2) how they differ, and (3) what they indicate about the next steps in group development.

At a later time a second evaluation might be made, with a comparison to determine where persons feel the staff has moved in the interim.

If the church is a body, then its staff will continue to change as the body changes. Each period in the life of the congregation will require the same thoughtful, prayerful consideration of mission and its effect on staff deployment as the first. Persons should not be recruited to fill established positions, but to complete the ministry for that time and place.

I.C.A.M. Team Development Wheel

Instructions: Place a mark on the circumference of the wheel to represent the present status of your team.

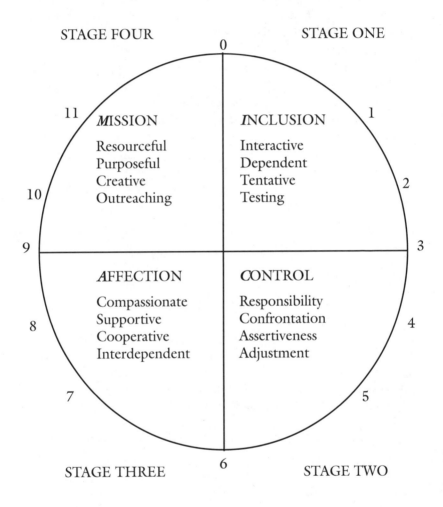

STAGE FOUR   0   STAGE ONE

11 *M*ISSION   *I*NCLUSION 1

Resourceful   Interactive
Purposeful   Dependent
Creative   Tentative 2
10 Outreaching   Testing

9   3

*A*FFECTION   *C*ONTROL

Compassionate   Responsibility
Supportive   Confrontation
8 Cooperative   Assertiveness 4
Interdependent   Adjustment

7   5

STAGE THREE   6   STAGE TWO

Team Spirituality: A Guide for Staff and Church by William J. Carter. Copyright © 1997 by Abingdon Press. Reprinted by permission.

Responding to New Roles

Each time a new person is to be added or someone leaves, the roles of all those on the staff are subject to reassessment and redeployment. Since we understand the staff to be a "system," we must see it as a constantly changing entity. For some staff persons that may seem very threatening. For some it might be. No doubt Barnabas and John Mark found the circumstances surrounding the redirection of the mission to the Gentiles a distasteful episode (Acts 15:36-41). But there are reassuring factors as well, if the church is truly a body. Both Barnabas and John Mark found other areas of ministry (1 Cor. 9:6; Col. 6:10; 1 Pet. 5:13), and the Pauline mission was enhanced by new roles and relationships. Periodic reconsideration of staff responsibilities need not be a threat if we remember several principles of ministry.

The first is that *gifts are not limited by roles*. The gift which brings a person into a staff may be practiced in a number of different areas of the life of the congregation. The same talent for good organization that made a person a great building manager may also make him or her an excellent program director. A Christian educator might become the director of lay ministries or cell groupings. The gift of caring response that earned the receptionist the goodwill of the entire congregation may become the foundation for a new role in the assimilation of new church members. The pastor who has done most of the hospital calling may find that someone else can do that task (with appropriate preparation of the congregation) while he or she takes on a new role as a source of vision and planning. Although some needs will persist (building maintenance) and some persons may not be able to move readily between roles (an age-level worker) and some skills are so specific it is hard to transfer them (organ playing), it is surprising to find that many congregations have found ways to adapt tasks to persons, as well as persons to tasks as they change their mission or structure.

The second is that *many persons have more than one gift.* When we work with persons for a while, we discover that the aptitude that first brought them to our attention is not always the one that makes them the most useful in the life of the body. There are times when proper staff function reveals obscured abilities that can be used in a new configuration. There are even persons who "can do almost anything." One of the tasks of the staff director or staff-parish committee is to discover the spectrum of gifts of staff persons so that they may be more wisely used, and protected when there are staff deployment changes.

Third, *it is possible to redefine position descriptions* so as to include the skills of some persons already on the staff. Even a new position may have characteristics so similar to some aspects of existing ones that a change of title and role will not be uncomfortable. It is not necessary to give up good qualities in a person just because a new direction is being charted for the staff overall.

When a dynamic new pastor came to Second Church, the decision was made by the board to move from a maintenance mode (keeping the old program and facilities going) to a growth mode. But the staff had all been hired to fulfill the objectives and values of the maintenance paradigm. The temptation was to fire everyone and hire new persons.

But a sensitive pastor and an understanding board created a different climate. The board asked the pastor, personnel committee, and staff to meet together to examine the new mode and how staff objectives might be defined and performed in the future. It was soon apparent that some of the present staff were already attuned to the new design and could easily be retrained. The associate pastor became the minister of outreach, the secretary's role was changed to church communicator with public relations and newcomer contacts, and a part-time office person was added. The choir director, who already had some skills and could learn others, was made the worship director, with responsibility for upgrading the service to meet the expectations of visitors as well as members.

The Christian educator felt that the new environment would not be challenging and applied for a job in another city. The facilities manager's responsibilities were changed so much that the incumbent did not care for the new role and took another job in the community. Both were replaced with one full-time person to serve as the coordinator of fellowship and spiritual growth, with specific responsibility for small-group and large-group formation. That completed the basic staff reconfiguration. More changes were made as the church grew and new staff were added, but each stage was accomplished with the same care as the first.

Fourth, *persons can be trained or retrained* to fit new staff job descriptions, even if their old skills are not sufficient. The giftedness persons bring may not reside in their specific capabilities but in their personalities or relational abilities. The organ player mentioned earlier may be a great leader of young adults if properly refocused and trained.

Finally, *there may be times when persons no longer fit* the profile of the staff the church now needs. In such cases there must be a process of preparation, separation, and continuing care that will enable the former staff person to enter a new setting and assume new responsibilities without loss of self-esteem or community support. Such separations are never without pain, but they may be managed without long-term damage by a loving and compassionate staff and congregation.

If the church is a body it will continue to adjust itself to its changing needs and challenges, but constant change may be too confusing. There are certain times in the life of a congregation when it is more appropriate and less threatening to reexamine the staff system for realignment. Using these times can be a strategic advantage. Some of these are:

1. When a staff person leaves for another job or community, or receives a new call or appointment. Any opening is an opportunity to look at all assignments.

2. During a revisioning or long-range planning process. If changes in mission or program are envisioned it will be helpful to include possible staff reassignments, additions, or replacements. In that way plenty of time is allowed for adjustments.

3. In a changing community (if the population is growing older or younger, if racial composition is changing, if suburbs are replacing farms, etc.), a change in staff may be indicated.

4. When pastoral leadership changes. There are different styles and skills among pastors. What one does well another may not do at all. The entrepreneurial pastor may either do it all or direct how it will be done, while the participative pastor will expect staff persons (and others) to be involved in all decision making. Each may have a different set of priorities. This may be a good time to look at jobs and time commitments.

5. As growth occurs, numerical or in program emphases. More people or program may mean more staff, or restructured roles, or conversely, more laity in ministry and less paid staff.

6. Financial exigencies. Less money, or more, can quickly revise estimates of the number and types of staff persons needed, although it is important to remember that the ability to pay is not the basic determinant of how much staff to have. *(Mission always determines staff definition.)* Resources only regulate the proportion of salaried to volunteer personnel.

Some church administrators say that staff costs will almost always take more than 50 percent of the budget, perhaps even as high as 80 percent in the next decade *(unless we rediscover the power of the ministry of the laity)*.

7. Relocation or remodeling. The building of a gym or a new education building can drastically change time requirements for some staff, and perhaps call for new personnel or reassessment of some staff responsibilities.

8. When tasks are not being performed adequately. The solution may be to change ways of doing things rather than staff, but it could also mean new persons and new tasks. This may be another time when the gifts of the members ought to become the focus of the effort of the whole body.

The Body of Christ is an organism. It fluctuates with the conditions around it, according to its inner health and vitality (spirituality) and in terms of the pressures upon it. Members of the congregation and members of the staff are part of the body, waxing and waning with it. At each juncture the health of the body and relationship between the parts of the body may need to be diagnosed and a treatment prescribed so that the whole body will stand a better chance of spiritual or physical growth.

Midstream Adjustment

Mostly, though, we find ourselves joining a staff that has already been formed. When that happens we have a lot of learning to do in a short time. Both senior pastor and staff persons (new or old) have responsibilities in developing the condition under which the ministry of the church can continue unabated until it can be reassessed and revitalized.

For the new *senior pastor* there are some actions that will provide a place to start on staff development. If I were being appointed or called to be the pastor of a staffed church, I would take at least the following steps:

1. I would read a couple of good books on multiple staffs. (Two suggestions: Lyle Schaller, *The Multiple Staff and the Larger Church* [Nashville: Abingdon Press, 1986]; and Anne Marie Nuechterlein, *Improving Your Multiple Staff Ministry* [Minneapolis: Augsburg, 1989].)

2. I would talk to my predecessor about the configuration of the staff, about the origins of staff job descriptions, and about the ways staff persons have related to one another on the job.

3. I would call a meeting of the staff, all of them, at which the main agenda would be gaining an understanding of what each feels he or she is supposed to be doing, along with an exploration of how they feel collectively about the vision that the church has for itself and where they feel they fit into it.

4. I would arrange for a *personal interview* with each staff person, at which time they would share individual perceptions of the mission of the church, and the call they felt made them want to be a part of it. Each would be asked to share dreams and hopes for the future of the church, and any barriers or insecurities they feel may prevent the fulfillment of that dream, as well as personal and spiritual needs.

5. I would meet with the church personnel committee and get their feelings about the staff, its configuration, and its performance. In the light of the scriptural understanding of the ministry of the body, I would make a special plea that they be open to interaction with me and the staff as we develop our ministry together. Church people want quality leadership but disagree on what quality is. Changing definitions of quality change the church. The personnel committee, the pastor, and the staff must define quality so that staff will know where to aim, and what ammunition to use.

6. I would prepare a brief, written description of staff roles and responsibilities based on what I heard, and share that with the whole staff, being sure to avoid any personal references or breach of confidence. I would then ask the staff to correct for accuracy, and *suggest any new ways of working that*

would improve total staff function, as well as more accurately reflect the mission of the church as we understand it.

7. I would set a schedule for a weekly staff meeting, with varying agendas, that would continue the process of sharing ministry, exploring spirituality, adopting desirable changes, and developing any new standards or directions, as well as managing the day-to-day life of the church. More on staff meetings in chapter 4.

8. I would adopt an attitude of support and mutuality of ministry toward all staff, to be maintained at all costs except harm to the church and its ministry. Staff need to know that the senior pastor is friend and advocate, as well as evaluator.

Some Suggestions for New Staff Persons

New staff persons also need to be aware that joining a group that continues in ministry involves more than showing up for work on time (although that may not be a bad idea), especially if the staff position is new, is different from the one previously held, or involves a change in job description for the congregation. If I were joining an existing staff as a new member I would:

1. Be sure that I have received a clear statement of expectations from the committee that hired me, and from the senior pastor or other supervisor. Written statements are good, but at times the specific definition of the task may be awaiting the experience of a trial ministry. Ask for clarity at any point where there seems to be ambivalence.

2. Ask for a time when I can discuss with the senior pastor his or her understanding of the task and role expected of me, and in which I can share understandings of ministry and the call.

3. If it is not offered I would suggest that I would like to have time in a staff meeting or retreat to hear other staff members talk about their perceptions of the mission and ministry of the congregation, and the roles and functions

each feels he or she has in that ministry. I would expect to share my own feelings if and when appropriate.

4. I would establish some work patterns that demonstrate discipline and commitment to the task, possibly in consultation with others.

5. I would engage laypersons I work with in conversations about ministry and the call, and ask their assistance in defining my role in ways that would be most helpful to the mission of the church.

6. I would develop a continuing relationship with some group in the church other than the staff (Sunday school class, circle, fellowship, spiritual search group) and allow them to be a part of my spiritual and social growth experience.

7. I would seek and accept feedback from the constituencies I serve and make sure that they know that I am trying to respond as a mature Christian to any new directions or behaviors that offer greater opportunities for ministry.

8. I would define personal time and use it carefully to maintain my own physical, social, and spiritual energies.

As senior pastors, staffs, and congregations examine their own roles in God's plan and develop a common understanding of the meaning of ministry and the mission of the body of which they are a part the way is open for growth in many directions. We will look at some of those in the next chapters.

CHAPTER THREE

Administering the Gifts

A New Perspective on Staff Management

Administering a staff is never easy. There are so many variables, and the expectations of constituents and coworkers are often so quixotic that evaluation and redirection appear to be necessary on an almost daily basis. The key is to understand the expectations and respond with gifted ministries. Understanding begins with the congregation itself.

Perception and Paradox: Understanding the Larger Church

Many of the staff of a larger church (any church with more than 500 members or 200 average attendance), including the senior pastor, will have come from smaller church settings, or will have failed to notice some characteristics of larger churches that may rise up and smite them as time goes on. Lyle Schaller has helpfully identified some of these, many of which have implications for staff selection and administration.

The Larger the Congregation:

1. The more difficult it is to enlist sufficient lay volunteers and the more need there is for a *systemic process* of securing, coordinating, and training lay volunteers in ministry. That is a surprise for most of us. We thought the opposite.

2. The greater the demand that the leaders initiate ministry and activities. Visioning, innovation, and planning by staff and a very few elected leaders is often assumed. Involvement of laity in the process is both *more difficult* and *more necessary*. A conundrum!

3. The more crucial it is for the pastor and congregation to recognize that pastor and staff can no longer be the shepherd to everyone, and the more necessity there is for planning carefully for congregational care. It will not happen spontaneously, and the staff cannot do all of it. But it must happen.

4. The more important it is to have a systematic and redundant communications system. Tell them, remind them, and tell them again! There are few post office or coffee shop networks in the larger church.

5. The greater inclination there is for congregational leaders to focus on property and financial matters instead of the ministry to which God is calling the congregation. The staff is often expected to carry the ministry torch.

6. The more vulnerable the church is to unexpected changes, including changes in pastor and staff. Rumors surge, indignation ignites. The more members there are the less they know, and the less members know the more they say.

7. The greater the dependence for stability and continuity on staff leadership and the group life of the church (especially the worship services) and the need for more disciplined planning of every event and program.

8. The more extensive is the dependence on staff and the higher the expectation that the senior pastor will be a good executive director. Roles are more general and functions broader, which means that they are more difficult to administer and more time will be involved for the administrator.

9. The more strategically important it is to use both small group and large group models in program development.

10. The more requirement there is for a decision-making structure that emphasizes performance and accountability.

11. The greater the temptation to substitute community service and congregational diversion for Christian witness and spiritual growth.

12. The greater the need for longevity in both staff tenure and program processes. Acceptance grows slowly and declines reluctantly.

(Selected and adapted from Schaller, *The Multiple Staff and the Larger Church* [Nashville: Abingdon Press, 1986], pp. 17-27.)

Spending time with staff reviewing and evaluating these observations, adding others from their experience in the local church, and rating how well the staff responds to these insights will raise the consciousness of the group that this is a whole new ball game.

The Paradox of Staff Performance

To understand these characteristics is to see the dimensions of the task of administering the gifts. Many of them indicate the reluctance of members of larger churches to accept responsibility for ministry, to seek evidence of giftedness, and to employ their own gifts in the ministry to which they are called as a body. This leads to a great paradox:

The more the staff members meet these expectations of the larger church the more popular and accepted they will be. But— the better the staff is at meeting these expectations the less likely it is that the larger congregation will ever learn to discover and embody its own ministry.

Dealing with this paradox will be a theme to which we will be called again and again in congregational ministry. Since the ultimate responsibility of staff is to shape the body into the image of Christ, its head, it will always have to deal with the limitations of the body to see its own higher interests, and the limitations of the staff in separating its own images of perfection from the vision to which God is calling it.

However, the responsibility of both pastor and staff for leading toward deeper spirituality and broader ministry should not interfere with the concurrent obligation to serve the present body with care and compassion. Many pastorates and staff relationships are marred by an unwillingness to minister to persons as they are while they are waiting to be transformed by the power of God into a new body. Impatience and disdain are not the ingredients of true ministry. *(We are servants before we are innovators.)*

Staff and Senior Pastor Expectations of One Another

I have encouraged pastors and local church staff persons and hundreds of members of seminars on multiple staff ministry to define their expectations of one another. There is enough similarity in the characteristics given to be able to provide a summary of what staff persons expect of a senior pastor and what senior pastors expect of staff persons.

What Staff Members Expect of Senior Pastors

1. The first expectation in almost every setting is that the pastor *model and encourage a good spiritual life.* Clearly, members of staffs do not expect the pastor to be perfect, but they do want him or her to be spiritually aware and active in a personal search for the will of God, and to support them in fulfilling their spiritual needs.

2. The second is like unto it: *The senior pastor should demonstrate trustworthiness, honesty, and integrity.* The whole staff process is undermined without these qualities in its leader. They are strongly emphasized almost everywhere.

3. Staff members expect a senior pastor to *support them in the ministries to which they are called or assigned.* Nearly always,

the discussion that follows includes references to understanding, advocacy, fair representation to boards and committees on personnel, protection from unfair critics, and personal consultation on working conditions and remuneration.

4. Staff persons want pastors to *know what ministry they expect of staff and be able to help set goals, clarify job descriptions, and deploy staff in the most effective way.* Very few staff persons want to be left on their own. They feel the need for a cooperative ministry, and expect the senior pastor to provide guidance in achieving it.

5. Senior pastors should *be available,* be willing to listen, and know how to assist communication between staff persons, and between staff and congregation. An "open-door policy" is implied, with a clear expectation that someone will listen. In addition, the staff expects the pastor to be responsive to their needs and helpful in their relationships with others. Staff know that the pastor is the key to congregational understanding of staff function.

6. They should exercise appropriate leadership by *developing and sharing a vision of how the whole ministry fits together.* The pastor is not expected to produce the whole vision for the church (staff and congregation hope to participate in the visioning process), but he or she is the only one who can tie it all together for the staff. "Administration is doing things right. Management is doing the right things," and "leadership is the development and articulation of a shared vision" (Lovett Weems, Jr., *Church Leadership, Vision, Team, Culture and Integrity* [Nashville: Abingdon Press, 1993], p. 34).

7. The senior pastor *should understand and claim his or her own gifts and ministry as a part of the total team.* Two strands are discernible: The pastor should know what he or she is called to do (and what he or she can do), and should know what others can do or do better than the pastor. Understanding of one's own ministry, and limitations, underlies the deployment of others.

8. They should *develop a plan for evaluation based on the*

performance of ministry and administer it equitably. Many staff express concern that evaluation is episodic, often based on factors unrelated to ministry and conducted in an unprofessional manner by committees or administrators. They feel that the pastor can help to see that fairness prevails. But, they do want to be evaluated, with opportunity to adjust to new expectations and modify behaviors before final decisions are reached about their effectiveness.

9. The pastor is expected to *protect personal and family time for self and staff* and see that social needs of staff are addressed. The pastor must model a commitment to time apart from work for personal relationships and renewal. (In one work-addicted staff we developed a rule that required posted staff itineraries to include at least one day a week reserved for personal and family time.) In addition, he or she sets the tone for staff social interactions. One person said, "There is no way for us to have fun together unless the pastor is in favor of it."

10. Finally, the pastor is expected to be *open to change and encourage openness in others,* both staff and congregational members. Flexibility and change are important to good ministry. The pastor is the primary model for styles of change and the most important guarantor that they will happen.

There are other items. In some places more emphasis is placed on the expectation for salary advocacy, the delegation of work and authority, time management, arranging office space, compassion, patience, and other issues, but staff mostly agree on the major items. In general, pastors seem to be content with the list, although somewhat surprised at its comprehensive nature, and willing to see it used as an evaluative tool.

What Senior Pastors Expect of Staff Members

In both multiple staff workshops and clergy seminars on staff development, I gather lists of the expectations of staff performance by senior pastors. These too have many similarities, and it is fairly easy to find the most desirable characteristics from the items presented at various times and places. The following list is a summary of pastors' feelings:

1. *Persons should have a sense of call to ministry* and *a willingness to negotiate its application to the position.* Most clergy accept the idea that both clergy and laity are called to ministry. All of them hope that the acceptance of a job includes a sense of call—but they would like to have an opportunity to talk with persons about the application of that call in a particular situation. The call cannot supersede the job description. No matter how strong a person's call to ministry may be, it may not fit the tasks or mission of a particular local church.

2. *Staff members should be team players.* In nearly every discussion of staff interaction there is considerable attention to this expectation. Staff members feel that it is vaguely threatening. Senior pastors explain that it is a sports analogy, which simply means that persons are expected to work together and do their share of the total ministry. A failure to accept individual responsibility or complete tasks is injurious to all, and "showboating" is pernicious. Team members support one another and cheer one another on. They accept direction and practice discipline. They are concerned with the ministry of the whole body, not just their assignment.

3. *Persons are expected to have competence.* It is not enough merely to have a vague sense of commitment. Staff persons are expected to know how to do what they are called or asked to do or to be willing to take training to learn the required skills. They should be gifted or trained in special ways that serve the special needs of persons.

4. *Staff persons are expected to be Christian together.* A "live" faith is assumed. Persons without a sense of Christian commitment are difficult to absorb into a staff setting. The observance of moral and ethical principles is a part of the basic standards of work in the local church, and awareness of the spiritual reality of the indwelling Christ enriches every act and relationship. Every

person, including the senior pastor, must be a servant leader—
servant of Christ and servant of the people of God.

5. *One of the often expressed expectations of staff is that they
be people-oriented.* Staff must reflect the attitude of Jesus,
which puts people first. Human relations skills are vital. Personal preferences or professional standards must take second
place to the needs of people. Helping the people to meet
God is the real objective, not some criteria related to traditional practices, denominational norms, or vocational goals.

6. *Loyalty is expected of staff persons.* Again, there are usually
some requests for explanations of this expectation. But the
primary focus is on loyalty to the staff, to the church, to the
ministry to which they are called, and to the senior pastor as
the staff director. Those who undermine any of these may
bring the whole structure down. Confidences must be kept.
A positive attitude must be expressed. Differences should be
worked out person to person.

7. *Those who occupy a position are expected to exercise creativity in the area for which they are responsible.* Being hired as a
staff person assumes that personal initiative will be a primary
motivational force. If a staff person has to be told what to
do, his or her value is greatly diminished. Staff persons need
to be self-starters, generating ministry.

8. It is fair to expect that *staff persons should be diligent
and productive.* People need to be on time. Things need to
get done. The urge to excellence is assumed. Everyone is
expected to be engaged in a quest for quality. When quality
improvement factors are identified, staff persons should
respond to them enthusiastically.

9. *Persons are expected to work under supervision and accept
evaluation.* No one is a law unto himself or herself. Everyone
is subject to a feedback system. Responsive change is
assumed. Those who will not hear cannot serve successfully.

10. *Openness and flexibility are essential to staff function.*
As circumstances change roles change. Tasks undergo redefi-

nition and redirection. Persons must be willing to participate in the changes necessary for continued effective ministry.

Other characteristics receive some attention: collegiality, being focused on task, honesty, having appropriate ambition—but the senior pastors tend to agree on the large areas. Most staff persons, after some reflection, seem to accept these criteria. They too are willing to be evaluated on these standards.

> It may be worthwhile for each staff to spend some time making its own list of expectations: staff of senior pastor and senior pastor of staff. Such an exercise can help all parties achieve a better relationship. Or the expectations listed above can be used as an aspect of the staff's evaluation of itself, with each person rating the achievement of the staff and senior pastor by these standards. In either case, the discussion that follows the use of the lists is the real benefit.

With openness and flexibility the whole staff can come to a better understanding of the way it works and how it might do better. Constant improvement, one of the goals of the Total Quality Management process, is the only way a staff can maintain its momentum.

Joining the Local Church

Unstated in both of these lists is a factor that may be more important than all the others in developing effective ministries with a congregation. It applies to pastor and staff alike. As more than one commentator has suggested, the most important shift for the pastor or staff person is to "join the local church," to become a physical and emotional member of the body in which his or her ministry is taking place. The congregation comes before denominational emphases, personal program projections, or individual priorities.

Pastor and staff must seek to build the spirituality of *this* group and bring *this* body into the ministry to which God is calling it. The vision from God for this congregation, the good of the people of this community, the development of the gifts of these people, is the purpose of spiritual leadership. The most destructive thing that any person can do to a local body of Christ is to pour it into a mold designed for another body, one that does not fit its own purpose and design.

Even if staff persons are members of another congregation or denomination they are useful only if they make the church they serve their primary ministry environment during the time they are employed. Even more important, they will need to invest their spiritual energies and personal vision in the local body, and work for its health and vitality. One must first love the church before he or she can reform the church.

Administering the Gifts

In one seminar for multiple staff churches, a participant remarked that the expectations of senior pastors and staffs for each other could be summed up in three words: *affirmation, respect,* and *spirituality.* Most of the rest of this book will be devoted to examining the process by which staff persons may relate to one another and to the congregation in ways that provide these essential elements.

There is a continuing responsibility for the daily oversight and spiritual development of those who work together in ministry as employees of a congregation. While all administration is a joint exercise, and each person has responsibility to see that it works, a particular responsibility is placed on the administrator. The person who carries the vision of the ministry of the church is the most effective one to administer its staff. In most local churches that is the senior pastor.

But what if the pastor's gifts do not fit into an administrative role? What if his or her operational mode is not compatible with the expectations of the staff and congregation for pro-active supervision? By the time pastors are called or appointed to the larger churches or judicatory offices it is assumed that they have the skill and inclination for administering the staff and its work. That is not always so. Some are at that level because of outstanding gifts which are unrelated to administration, or even because there is no one else available. Some are able preachers and have been called or appointed to "larger pulpits." Some are good pastors and have been brought in to heal wounds and bring unity. Some are effective promoters, whose reputations have been built on the ability to energize and build up a congregation. Some are competent practitioners, who do what they do well, but bring little creativity or innovation to staff development. How can they meet the challenge of administration?

They can enter management skills training (staff development seminars are one type of training). Sometimes ineffectiveness is a product of inexperience. It may be rooted in habits formed in situations where there was no one else to depend on, or where the pastor was expected to be the whole show. Different abilities and leadership styles may be required for the new administrator than were needed to manage the unstaffed church. Skills training can help.

They can turn to the pastor/personnel committee or the administrative board. Although the strongest staffs usually have a strong administrator, governing boards can be more effective than we sometimes think, if they are given the tools and the authority. They are capable of taking on a lot of responsibility, including some oversight of a staff. In some congregations experienced laypersons are available who can assume some management tasks with great effectiveness in part-time or volunteer positions.

Sometimes it may be possible to add a staff manager to the roster to take care of some details. The staff manager can be either a layperson or a clergyperson. A number of churches are now experimenting with the use of a designated staff person as the administrator. Although reports from the first experiences are positive, it will be a long time before the practice becomes general, and it will usually be in churches with many staff persons. Whatever the result, each pastor and board will have to make its own decision, based on criteria peculiar to the parish.

> I became aware of two pastors who felt no aptitude or inclination for administering the staff. Both staffs were asking for more direction and both pastors were frustrated. In less than a year one of the pastors (of a very large church) left the ordained ministry.
>
> The other enlisted the staff and the board in a process of understanding his call and ministry, making adjustments that allowed others to take charge of some functions. He is entering his fourth year of effective ministry to that congregation.

Even more fundamentally, our gifts paradigm implies that one reason for poor management results is that we do not engage the congregation and the staff in the ministry they are called to do, nor do we provide direct spiritual resources for the staff and congregation. Not just the staff, but the whole body is the source for ministry formation and leadership. The administration of staff may be seen as a process of bringing the parts of the body into conformity with its head, Jesus Christ (spirituality), rather than initiating some current administrative methodology borrowed from secular management environments.

Help Define and Claim Gifts

One of the basic functions of staff administration in the gifts paradigm is to help persons define and claim their ministry. This role is crucial in both recruitment and administration. Not only must senior pastors be aware that possibilities for additions to the ministry staff are all around them, they also must be aware that those presently serving may be handicapped by the lack of attention given to bringing gifts to maturity.

Some very talented persons are less effective than they should be because they are being consumed with tasks that they feel are not central to their call, or because they are doing what they feel called to do in a situation where the expectations are for a different function. The pastor may feel that much time will be wasted in going over the feelings of each staff person in individual interviews. But respect for the gifts of others calls us to go the extra mile in the discovery of true gifts. It is more likely that the time used here will save hours or days that would be required later in frustrating attempts to straighten out what has become hopelessly snarled in emotional interactions between the staff person, his or her constituency, and the board, not to mention strained relationships between the pastor and the staff person.

There are some adjustments that may help persons to express their ministry more fully. Alterations can be made in total staff assignments so that more compatible tasks can be lodged with persons who enjoy them or feel called to do them. The secretary who does not feel qualified to design the newsletter might well exchange that task with the musician who would like another outlet for creativity but hates to file the choir music folders. The secretary could do the filing, and both persons would be more content (for a while at least). When tasks are separated from roles (designing the newsletter is a task, "secretary" is often a role) and the theology of the gifts is applied, it is possible to find many ways to relieve tension and increase compatibility. A good administrator does everything possible to free up persons to express their gifts in ministry.

In addition, some persons are occupying positions because they feel a general sense of the need to be in ministry and their staff position was the only place open to them at the time for service in a church setting. A sensitive administrator can help discover the focus of the call and guide persons into the proper channels of preparation for a truer expression of the gifts.

The pastor of a three-church parish was frustrated and ineffective. Both he and his people were unhappy. An insightful pastor of a nearby large church invited the floundering pastor to become his associate. As the relationship matured there was opportunity to explore the actual call the younger man felt. As a result he took a leave of absence from the staff and enrolled in a Christian education curriculum. Upon graduation he obtained a position in another church as a minister of Christian education, an assignment in which he showed great gifts. He continues to grow in that ministry.

A secretary in a United Methodist district office served the job well but began to feel the call to another form of ministry. With the sympathetic understanding and support of the superintendent, she became a candidate for ordained ministry, entered seminary, and is now serving a local church as pastor.

At the very least an administrator who is aware of the nature of gifts can make every effort to see that some provision is made to allow a person in any staff position to do tasks that express giftedness.

One of my many mistakes was feeling that the secretary of a congregation that I served was wasting her time talking to many persons on the phone each day about their ailments, insecurities, and concerns. After much discussion and some tense moments, I finally began to realize that her work was saving me a lot of time—and that she had a real knack for caring about another person's feelings. We arranged for volunteers to answer the other phone lines while she continued to do a great job with the secretarial duties and her counseling.

Sometimes a feeling of being in ministry is greatly enhanced if routine tasks can be supplemented by more clearly ministry-centered interactions. A vital consideration here is that we must not forget that *the whole congregation is an extended staff,* that gifts are everywhere, and that a big part of our role is to see that someone is exploring the meaning of the gifts with all the people and helping them to be in ministries that express their Christian calling and concern. Even as we work as a staff we need to be reminding persons of the nature of the gifts and calling them to minister, including the provision of discovery and support mechanisms that will encourage the formation of ministry units.

The pastor, staff, and congregation are united in the gifts process. A whole ministry comes from the whole body, a spiritual organism regulated by Christ at its head. The freedom of the concept of the gifts and the body cannot be overestimated. For the administrator who genuinely believes that all are called to ministry, and who has taken the time to prepare the members of the body for the ministries to which they are called and gifted, the possibilities for sharing ministry are endless. And there are no distinctions. All of the tasks of discipleship are open to all persons, clergy and laity. Finally, Luther's doctrine of "the priesthood of all believers" is coming to fulfillment (although Luther himself never favored full application of his own best insight). When we use the gifts and functions as the basis for all administration, the church is freed to become a true body and its staff to become dynamic parts.

Helping Persons Out

Persons are not hired to do the bidding of the pastor or even to satisfy a job description, but to assist in the ministry of the church. They need freedom to explore and organize their ministry functions in ways that will be best suited to their call and style of operation. If, however, the tasks needed to continue the ministry to which the body feels that it is called are not being completed expeditiously, the pastor is responsible for discovering a way to see that performance is improved. Gifts administration, like Total Quality Management, is interactive, not punitive. The objective is to do a better job.

It is even possible that depth discussions may uncover the long-suppressed knowledge that the local church is not the best place for ministry, either because the call was not really there or because the gifts do not fit the environment. In such cases the administrator can help with an exit process that preserves self-respect and points the direction to a new place of service. After all, God calls persons to secular employment as well as to work in the church. There should be no stigma if individuals move from one to the other.

Many church managers have learned that most discussions about job performance come down to the phrase "yarelyotta-wanna." That is, the staff person really ought to want to do what the supervisor wants done. But ministry is not so easy to pin down. It is a system, with its own set of rules and variables. We must discover its components together and try to work out a mutually acceptable process, including reorganization or retraining. If that is not possible then we need to seek a compassionate way to find another arena of ministry for that person. Inability to perform the basic expected ministry as a part of staff threatens the performance of the whole staff. Part of the responsibility of the administration of the gifts is to see that the failures of one do not jeopardize the ministry of all (remember John Mark?). The way out may be as important as the way in. Both the ministry and the staff person need to be protected from each other's failures.

Self-Renewal Time

Gifts administration requires that leaders protect time for self, family, and spiritual renewal. The gifts decay in an environment of stress or estrangement. Since the true context of all the gifts is love (see 1 Corinthians 13) and love flows out of the serene, overflowing heart, it is impossible for those who would achieve full effectiveness to live without the renewal of love.

During the last ten years we have seen televangelists, pastors of large churches, denominational executives, and bishops succumb to the ravages of overconcentration on success and personal goals. Families have been ignored, spiritual lives have been neglected, and the regeneration of the self has been replaced with self-indulgence. And more than one pastor of a large church has announced that he or she is leaving the ministry, bitterly complaining that it is too demanding, too destructive of family and personal life. It can be. It is self-destructive—unless gifts are managed with care and lives protected against the depredations of addiction to the institution, or self, and freed to express the gifts of ministry laid on by God.

Family and friends may be the first casualty of a life that is too "dedicated." The cultivation of relationships with those who love us, and with those whose presence sustains us, is one of the best shields against the pernicious radiation of the rays of guilt or ambition that drive some to frenzied activity. Not only clergy, but laypersons who work in the church, business leaders, professionals, and blue-collar employees are all subject to the loss of love and life in the spirit that follows when lives are allowed to become consumed with activity. The popularity of "Spiritual Formation" retreats, Family Life events, and Marriage Enrichment seminars attests to the need persons feel for a reimmersion in the core values of life.

Early detection and correction of the tendency to relate everything to work (wife and children in church because it helps the image of the pastor; playing golf to do business; using vacation time to construct sermons, or write that book, instead of building the quality of life in our family; constructing public prayers instead of praying) may prevent many later problems. The maintenance of self-esteem, self-confidence, and self-renewal is part of the structure of the life truly lived within the framework of the gifts. We are worthy, we can be assured, and we can re-create ourselves because God has given us the charge and the means to prepare ourselves for ministry at its best.

Paring Superfluous Organization

One of the most useful administrative roles is to ensure that staff persons are involved in ministry rather than debilitating and redundant meetings. A teacher once told me, "The church was born in a meeting, and without meetings it will die." That is another truism that has its pitfalls. Two of these are (1) we can spend so much time in meetings that there is no time left to do ministry, and (2) we may have taught many persons to count meeting attendance as ministry, and left the impression that a good attendance ensures success. We sometimes trumpet the attendance at the rally for evangelism and then discover that the actual number of persons involved in doing evangelism and the number of persons won are no greater than before. The meeting was substituted for ministry.

To gain control of meetings, the first necessity is to pare the organizational structure to its bare bones. In the past we have often encouraged organizational expansion as a way to involve persons. A little more reflection has led most of us to conclude that it is not more organization we need but more ministry: work groups and spiritual growth groups, not talk groups. (In some denominations and among the independent churches governing boards are often less than a dozen for a membership of thousands, but ministry groups abound.) Once the church has reached a consensus on its ministry focus its people should be freed to express whatever ministry within that context that flows from the gifts. Both pastor and staff should focus on ministry.

The organizational structure should be just enough to keep the church functioning and no more. That will cut down on the number of meetings, but there is more.

I can well remember months of pastorates when more than twenty planning meetings were scheduled during a thirty-day period (work areas, councils, committees, boards), and I felt that I or one of the staff members had to be at all of them. Only in the latter years of ministry did I finally realize that people could have meetings without us. *The pastor who thinks that he or she must be in every meeting (or have an appointed proxy) has already lost faith in the grace of giftedness.* Persons with gifts can be trusted to find the will of God for the ministries that will express them. Constant oversight is not required by some church "hired hand." The gifts free persons for ministry instead of constraining them. Of course some coordination is needed. Conflicting purposes and schedules can be confusing, but a coordinating group can handle that. There can be fewer meetings, and less involvement by administrators in the ones that remain, if we genuinely trust our people to find and express their gifts.

But we cannot just opt out of meetings and leave the laity to sit through the boring details. We must rethink the whole structural concept and reform it for ministry rather than deliberation. The organizational structure should be just enough to keep the church functioning and no more. The pastor is the key to building and maintaining an organization that serves ministry instead of a program to serve the organization.

An Exercise for Gifts Administration

In consultations with church staffs I have used a number of instruments to help them open discussion of their working relationships. One of these is the Checklist for Gifts Administration. You will note that many of the items correspond with points made in this chapter. To use the survey form follow these steps:

1. Have everyone on the staff fill out the form. Have someone collect copies of the forms and prepare totals for each item. (Be sure that each person retains his or her own.)

2. In a staff meeting or other setting give everyone a copy of the form with the totals on it. Also include an average for each item (totals divided by the number of forms. Compute to two decimal places—2.04, and so forth). Determine which are highest, lowest. Discuss why this may be true in each case.

3. Suggest that each person compare his or her own score on each item with the average for the whole group. Ask if anyone has a comment about the differences, if any. Give plenty of time for responses.

4. Engage the group in a discussion of what needs to be done to improve group performance and satisfaction. Start with the survey but allow items not on the form to be introduced and discussed.

5. Develop some goals for change or improvement that can be implemented and measured.

As stated earlier, use whatever you are comfortable with to involve the staff in learning conditions. Instruments and interactive processes are for opening discussions, not creating psychological profiles. Their best product is not in the person but in the group. Their validity is in the insight they bring to group process.

Checklist for Gifts Administration
for Staff Persons

Indicate your evaluation by putting
the number in the appropriate blank.

	Mostly (3)	Partly (2)	Hardly (1)
1. I know what my abilities/goals are.			
2. I know the expectations of my job.			
3. We have developed staff priorities.			
4. We get started on time and keep up.			
5. We undertake only what we can handle.			
6. We each understand the others' roles/jobs.			
7. We work at clarifying relationships/roles.			
8. I trust my coworkers to do their jobs.			
9. We keep up with routine responsibilities.			
10. We respond to inquiries promptly.			
11. We have adequate visioning and planning.			
12. We interact well as coplanners.			
13. We recover from interruptions satisfactorily.			
14. We respond well to complaint and criticism.			
15. We have time for personal lives and family.			
16. We are growing together spiritually.			
17. We meet the needs of our constituencies.			
18. Our meetings are worthwhile.			
19. I feel supported and appreciated.			
20. We have healthy personal relationships.			
TOTALS (add the numbers for each column.)			

AREAS WE NEED TO WORK ON: _____

Team Spirituality: A Guide for Staff and Church by William J. Carter. Copyright ©
1997 by Abingdon Press. Reprinted by permission.

CHAPTER FOUR

Building the Team

The Foundations

The primary role of the church is to ensure that (1) persons find resources for their spiritual needs (grow closer to Christ, the head), and (2) employ themselves in expressing that spirituality in ways that demonstrate the presence of God in the body and in the world. Both are necessary to avoid the twin imperfections of spiritual pride and trivial activities. As parts of the Christian body, the staff of the local church shares this role and is responsible for seeing that it is fulfilled.

That is not simple. The spiritual needs of persons are so varied and their paths to fulfillment so diverse that the identification of specific areas of application sometimes eludes even the best leaders. It will be our intention here and in the chapters to follow to suggest some ways in which the staff may approach the mediation of spiritual resources that will give access to all within the body.

Setting the Stage

For the staff itself spirituality is affected by interpersonal relationships. However conspicuous the spiritual expression of some staff persons may be, the impact on the congregation and the community will be determined by the perceived unity and teamwork evidenced by the members as they go about their tasks. For most people, the biblical standard that love for God is shown by love among persons still rules. The foundation of spirituality for staff is respect and affection among its members.

While some staffs may develop an immediate rapport and work together in effective harmony from the beginning, many others will find that differing backgrounds and work styles will cause some loss of momentum unless an inclusion process is instituted. Whether the core ministry of the church is assisted by three persons or three dozen, there will be times when the staff needs to focus on itself in order to develop the kind of dynamic that will encourage spiritual growth among the individual staff members and in the members of the congregation.

We have already discussed the exchange of information about roles and responsibilities, which is one way to get started on interpersonal understanding. In this chapter we will address the issue of team building more directly. However, I hope that no one will interpret the term only in its sports sense. We are not discussing here the formation of a group headed by a "coach" or manager dedicated to winning at any cost, or an arrangement that gives every person an assigned task that will result in a choreographed "play." In the church setting the team is a group of persons with a defined spiritual objective developing an operational style and process that will enable them to achieve fruition.

Team building is a series of activities that enables the team to discover its best operational style and maintain its process in order to fulfill its purpose and accomplish its objectives. Some of these activities are so elementary that it seems gratuitous even to mention them, but fundamentals are important.

Basic to all staff interaction is a dependable process that permits everyone to feel some confidence and security in the group. Spirituality flourishes in an atmosphere of trust. This includes four factors:

1. A regular staff meeting schedule
2. Simple operational protocols
3. Checkpoints for individual reassurance and redirection
4. An equitable employment policy

The Staff Meeting

The staff meeting is the single most important factor in maintaining relationships among staff persons and momentum in ministry. Over the years some people have denied this. Staff meetings have been labeled "boring" or "unproductive." One writer for a denominational publication called staff meetings a waste of time. But nothing can take the place of a well-prepared staff meeting. Which brings us to a key point: Good staff meetings do not just happen. They are designed.

A) Remember that a staff meeting can be the occasion for a variety of interactions: spiritual development, mutual support, sharing perceptions and experiences of ministry, calendaring, goal setting, problem solving, coordinating, evaluation of ministries, and interpersonal understanding. The list could go on. The secret is to develop a strategy for including appropriate general topics as well as current issues in a well-structured time frame.

B) Most staff meetings should include spiritual emphasis, coordination of program, and learning experiences. There is significant talk these days about being a learning organization to handle rapid change: Good staff meetings foster this kind of learning, so that change is perceived gradually, instead of suddenly.

C) The atmosphere of the staff meeting should be light, unhurried, and fun.

D) An agenda is vital to the meeting's effectiveness. Although any member of the staff may be responsible for coordinating the agenda, the chairperson is probably the best choice. The first consideration is the long-term plan for including appropriate topics for staff learning. Current matters can be scheduled as they occur. The whole agenda process might cover months.

The person coordinating the agenda should consult with other members of the staff to construct a basic agenda outline. At least a day prior to the meeting someone should check with staff members to see what topics need to be brought to the meeting. (Checking can be assigned to anyone, even a different person each time.) On days that few current issues are anticipated there is opportunity for more general topics. Once the meeting convenes, the group should approve or amend the agenda, then follow it faithfully. Time limits (previously adopted) should be rigorously observed unless the group agrees that emerging issues merit extension. When an issue threatens to dominate the meeting it may help to defer it to another time, perhaps to a special session for that purpose only.

E) Meeting patterns can vary. At one agency we had a full meeting every two weeks and a Work Assignment Meeting (WAM) on alternate Mondays. Full meetings were from one to two hours. (Not everyone was expected to stay the whole time every time.) In the WAM meeting we stayed on our feet and the only topic was work flow. In about five minutes we mentioned what materials or facilities needed to be prepared and when they were required so that the office staff and the program staff could coordinate time and production.

F) Retreats on special topics, and just for fun, are excellent resources. Retreats should be planned for the convenience of staff, and occasionally should include families if possible. Retreats may be for the entire staff or for groups specifically involved in decision making—but in the latter case results should be shared with all staff as soon as possible.

The staff meeting is the greatest ally of personal and spiritual growth for staff. Work on it!

Operational Protocol

A) Staff are responsible to one another. That means letting others know where we are and what we are doing when we are on duty. A simple in/out sheet in the church office or other method of sharing itineraries (such as on a local area computer network) ought to be standard. All personnel should be required to participate, including the senior pastor.

B) A standard mechanism for scheduling church facilities and equipment should be publicly available. Many congregations use computer scheduling programs. A large wall calendar will suffice. Appoint someone to be in charge. Keep the schedule current.

C) Establish a rule of confidentiality for all intrastaff communications, including staff meetings and other conversations, if church business or church members are involved or if personal matters are discussed.

D) The staff will operate as a team, making decisions by consensus whenever possible. In intractable situations, after every effort has been made to reach agreement and time for reflection has been allowed, the senior pastor will break the impasse, either by personal decision or vote of the group.

E) The team will set aside time to select goals and objectives for its own work periodically. Although not every activity needs to be included, there should be a clear understanding of the overall purpose of staff endeavor. Sharing these goals with the whole body through a bulletin or the church newsletter may be helpful.

F) Individual staff members should agree to submit all new program or procedural concepts to the entire staff before offering the concepts to groups for adoption or implementation. Each staff person should know what the others are doing. Valuable insights about possibilities and pitfalls may come from staff discussions. This is especially important to the support staff (office persons), because they are the ones most likely to get hard questions from parishioners.

G) Staff persons should be informed from the beginning that they are expected to provide supportive services and adjustments in their own areas to sustain strategies initiated by other staff persons and ministries approved by the programming and governing bodies of the church.

H) Once a new program or concept has been examined and put in place the entire staff should prepare to be supportive in public and candid in private. (Staff administrators should take special note.) Private conferences or staff meetings are the place to discuss results, problems, redesigns, and retrenchments. In public settings staff should express confidence and give affirmation. For example, when things are not going well the confidence expressed may be, "Oh, yes, Jill and the staff realize there are some problems, but we are confident that we can work through all of that." Or, "Greg knows about that and is looking for a solution. Don't be afraid to talk to him about it." The key is that the staff has shared ownership before the public questions occur.

Each staff will need to develop its own operational "shell," but it is vital that a process and policies be constructed that enable the staff to communicate freely about its work.

Checkpoints

In addition to staff evaluation and support, and an open-door policy for private conversations about personal or work-related subjects, staff need a clearly defined process for affirmation and feedback. One method is to schedule semiannual or quarterly sessions with each staff person for informal conversations about work satisfaction, performance, and prospects, separate from the annual evaluation. Questions to start the conversation might include:

1. How do you feel about your work right now?
2. What do you need from me (us) to help you?

3. What has made you feel the best about yourself recently?
4. Are there any improvements you should undertake?

These sessions tend to prevent the problem of some persons getting more praise (or blame) because they are assertive, while less assertive members go unnoticed. They also permit early notice of impending problems or desirable adjustments. (If reprimands or corrective behavior are given they should be put in writing and signed by both parties.) Not every administrator will like this particular method, but systematic checkpoints need to be built into staff routine.

> In one consultation with a troubled staff I had a conversation with one of the suspected troublemakers. When I asked this person about the tension she said, "I haven't felt that I had any respect from the pastor since I have been here. I don't think he understands what I do. I have asked for a conversation but he never has time to talk. I think we could work it out if we had some time together."
>
> One of the recommendations was to set up an interview schedule for all staff with the senior pastor. In a follow-up I learned that the situation had improved. It is certainly not always the senior pastor's fault when things go wrong, but he or she often holds the key to better relationships.

Employment Policy

A written policy on conditions and expectations for employment is increasingly important for legal reasons, but it has always been vital to staff comfort. While it is true that working conditions and remuneration rank low on the motivation chart for remaining in church vocations, they can quickly become first priority in any disagreement. Like any other worker, the church employee is entitled to know what the rules are in advance.

The policy statement should include responsibilities of the church and the employee, conditions of employment, work hours, holiday and vacation standards, performance evaluation procedures, termination and appeal provisions, and anything else that really matters. It should state general requirements as far as possible (i.e., criteria for vacation time should apply to all, with any exceptions noted and explained). Individual contracts based on the policy are highly desirable, with duties and essential functions outlined for each position or person. Some process should be initiated to be sure that persons have read both policy and contract and agree to the provisions before they are hired. The security of an equitable policy and administration can do wonders to free up persons to be spiritual leaders.

Some Team-Building Activities

An author contributed a pungent comment about team building to the consulting circuit, which I picked up from a friend who had it in his notes: "Teamwork occurs best when members work, worship and play or fight together, concerning some particular focus, rather than hearing lectures on how to be cooperative, considerate and responsible team members." I do believe that trust is acquired from working on a task of substance, rather than from sitting together in a meeting and hoping for more trust. So I like to use actual staff processes, interactive learning experiences, and routine interpersonal relations settings as opportunities for growth.

Team building means interactive improvement of skills and relationships, which fosters growth toward spiritual unity. Whatever contributes to the integration of these elements of staff development eventually makes ministry more effective. Some of these activities are interpersonal interactions, some are extensions of normal professional processes, and some use instruments (focused surveys) to assist interpersonal understanding.

Interpersonal Interactions

Fundamental to the life of the body is affection. Unlike many industrial environments, which shun familiarity between management and workers, the church operates entirely within a context of love. Whatever nourishes Christian affection helps the body fulfill its purpose. Social and interpersonal interactions that bring persons closer together are intrinsic to the life of the body. For staff that is doubly true. Trips, games, parties, worship experiences, conversations, meals, family gatherings, and other social opportunities are part of the bonding process, whether in the normal course of events or in retreat settings. However, let me issue two warnings: first, care should be observed to plan inclusive activities that all can enjoy; and second, bonding with each other should not become a barrier to participation in the larger body.

Extended Processes

In many churches the staff is not considered a part of the strategic planning core. The pastor and selected laypersons record the vision, select the objectives, and implement the plans, with the help of staff as assigned by pastor or board. However, it is becoming increasingly apparent that more involvement by staff is not only desirable, but necessary, if the church is to be renewed. Staff are a source of great ideas and can better support programs if they are part of the planning. More important for our theme, involving staff in the vision, objectives, and plans of the church helps them grow into a unified band. Staff play a vital role in at least four areas:

1. In developing a *methodology* for managing the program voted by the governing board, especially the role of the whole staff. A holistic approach to program implementation involves much interaction among staff and with others.

2. In generating *strategies for renewal* when the church becomes stalled by lethargy or conflicting purposes and cannot properly focus on revitalization. Church boards and members will need to be given voice and vote in the process, but someone has to start the process.

3. In *gathering* the strands of emerging vision and coordinating them for consideration by the body. Increasingly, administrators are seeing that no one can do a job in isolation. All are interdependent, and all are a part of the whole ministry of the body and part of its visioning team.

4. In *evaluating church facilities.* In this area the staff is more knowledgeable than anyone else and should be a part of the process of assessing, renovating, and designing buildings.

But what if some staff are uninterested, or feel incapable of participating in this level of planning and implementation? Such reluctance should be respected. Persons do know their limitations. However, the perspectives of just those employees may be the most vital link in projecting the whole picture. It often happens that when they are involved in the process at a level at which they feel comfortable they gain confidence and develop skills they did not know they had. Later involvement is easier and more effective.

The first staff I ever supervised was composed of me, a secretary, a building maintenance worker, and a part-time youth worker. We had a good informal relationship but hardly ever met as a group. We just talked in passing, or I gave orders (self-consciously and ineptly). One day the secretary brought lunch for the four of us, and we sat around the kitchen table chatting and eating. In an unexpected twist in the conversation we began to discuss the antiquated church building, which we all fretted about. Not only were the rooms badly arranged, but access to the sanctuary was from the wrong end. Topography was blamed for the failure to correct the problem.

The maintenance worker said meditatively, "You know, I've been thinking about that. If we knocked a hole in the wall where the back steps come down to the Sunday school rooms, and made an entrance there, we would have ground access to all the rooms and people could use that door to enter the sanctuary if they were late." After a few minutes of stunned silence we all saw the rationale of the plan. I took it to our local architect, who said it was feasible. Not only did we fix the entrance, we built a whole new education building that connected at that doorway.

From then on we had quarterly staff strategy sessions.

To illustrate this concept we will include here three staff interactions that will both help the ministry and build teamwork. All have implications for spirituality, affirmation, and trust in the staff and in the congregation. Each can be done in a long staff meeting or a retreat. (In some cases, with great care, appropriate leaders of the congregation may be included in the process.)

Constituency Identification and Quality Improvement

A) After explaining the meaning of constituency (in marketing jargon these groups are referred to as segments) ask each staff person to list the constituencies for which he or she feels special responsibility (i.e., Sunday school, youth group, trustees, newcomers, older adults, telephone callers) and rate how well he or she feels that constituency is served on a scale of one to five, with "1" meaning poorly served and "5" meaning well-served. (Rate with special attention to how well spiritual growth is supported.)

B) Compile the lists, making notations to show where more than one staff member claims the same constituency, and average the service rank numbers.

C) Discuss how staff members feel about service to those constituencies and specific improvements that could be made.

D) List any constituencies that did not get mentioned in the first round, examine why they were not included, and devise strategies for making quality improvements in those areas.

E) Compile the entire list. Identify feasible improvements and assign one or more staff persons to implement them. After a prayer together agree on a time for follow-up reporting.

Power Analysis and Support Design

A) At a time when a big change or changes are proposed in the ministry of the church set aside a time for the staff to do a "power analysis." The first step is to make a list of the individuals and/or groups whose approval and support are crucial to the implementation of this change. (For instance, a new worship pattern might need the support of the choir, Jim Walters, the John Knox Sunday school class, Gretta Parkins, the youth group, and the altar guild.) Remember, church members give opinions and complaints to *all* staff. Include all of them.

B) After a prayer for all the people of the church, and especially the individuals and groups who are being considered, do an analysis of why each person and group is important and whether each can be considered initially for or against the new proposal. Stay positive, but be candid.

C) Develop a design to provide support for the "pros" and persuasion for the "cons." Decide which information or appeal would be appropriate. Assign each person or group to a staff person or church member who has access to the individual or group. Move slowly, and provide reasoned support rather than manipulation.

D) One of the purposes of the analysis is to discover people's mood or reaction to the proposed change. If considerable resistance is encountered revision or postponement might be indicated. No change should be instituted by force.

E) If support seems to be growing, move toward consolidation. Openly acknowledge any remaining reluctance without identifying persons. (A brief statement will suffice. For example, "We know that not everybody agrees that this is the best plan.") Make a pact to reconsider if the new plan does not work out.

Issues Clarification and Strategic Planning

A) Before the meeting or retreat have each staff person make a list of what he or she feels are the three (or some other small number) most important issues facing the church at this time. Be sure that it is clear that "issues" means both opportunities and concerns. Include all staff. Some of the support staff may know more about issues than the program staff. As stated before, people talk to them.

B) Collate and rank the issues. Some may be interpersonal, some programmatic, some structural. Spend some time clarifying them to be sure everyone understands the real issue. Pray about the list. Select the most important issues for immediate attention. Record the others for later consideration (they must not be lost—some may turn out to be more vital than they seemed at first).

C) Develop a strategy to resolve one or more of these issues or bring them to the proper bodies (elders, deacons, board, trustees, and so on) in a form that will ensure attention and response. That may take considerable finesse. Renewal is not always a popular direction. There is a lot of emotional investment in the way things are.

D) After the first issues are launched begin with others. The whole church may catch the spirit and move forward, with ideas coming from everyone, or resistance to the first attempts may slow the whole process. Be adaptable but persistent.

There are dozens of ways to bring staff together in common experiences: congregational or personal problem-solving, dealing with criticism and complaint, developing focused spiritual life resources (more about this in the next chapters), addressing programmatic issues. With practice, staff will increase skills for dealing with issues and thereby shorten the amount of time required for addressing them.

Pastors have been known to bemoan the slowness of such planning methods and to express fear that early resistance among staff (and others) will scuttle the whole show. But "persons support what they propose," and if there is opposition it is much better to meet it early and openly rather than later and covertly. Staff persons have been known to complain that they cannot do their work and do the planning too. But much of the frustration of the work may be due to the failure of strategy. By using these and other techniques for whole staff involvement, we enable the staff to have some measure of control over its own destiny, involve staff members in intense working relationships, and provide opportunities for staff to build both self-confidence and solidarity.

Using Instruments

The staff can also benefit from the occasional use of various survey-type instruments that encourage personal interchange and self-disclosure. Some of the most well-known of these are the Myers-Briggs personality-type indicators, The Grid Management based tests, and group dynamics profiles. While some of these require professional certification to administer, similar instruments are available that may be used by anyone. The key is to understand that the use of such tests is not for scientific identification of psychological traits but for starting discussion.

They permit persons to talk about their own attributes and peculiarities, and those of others, without undue threat.

I have used, adapted, and developed a number of these instruments for use in seminars and local church consultations. Three of them are included here, with general directions for use. Your staff may want to spend a couple of hours in an extended meeting or retreat in "debriefing" one of them, or one of the dozens of others available.

Personal Tendencies and Leadership Styles

This is an attempt to provide an instrument based on daily life instead of just the work setting. The survey is found on pages 89-92.

A) Provide copies of the test section well ahead of time so that persons can work on them before the meeting.

B) Have everyone compile scores and transfer them to the "thermometers" by each style. Have them note the positive and negative qualities of each style. Point out that all styles are necessary for full function of a group, but that most persons predominate in one. That becomes their preferred style of operation. Each person may be different. It is the blend of the styles with the purpose of the group (situational leadership) that makes them effective.

C) Suggest that persons in turn "claim" the qualities of their predominant style (some may have a tie—do both) by stating which of the listed positive and negative traits they feel they actually have. If persons feel that the traits do not fit at all, ask them to give traits they think they have. (Limit each person's responses to two minutes.) Other members of the staff may affirm or question the identification, with responses by the one being "examined."

D) After all have had a turn (in large staffs this may take more than an hour), ask if they have learned anything about themselves or each other. Ask for examples.

E) Close by asking if there are leadership styles that the group lacks, and how to obtain them if they are needed.

Personal Tendencies and Leadership Styles

Place a 4 beside the statement with which you most agree in each section, 3 for the next, and so forth.

1. Life Plan
   ——— (a) The main thing in life is to get along with people.
   ——— (b) Life plans need to be made in consultation with others who are involved.
   ——— (c) Everyone ought to have a long-term plan for life.
   ——— (d) The best way to live is to take life as it comes.

2. Groups
   ——— (a) Most of the time, I take a visible leadership role in groups I am in.
   ——— (b) I tend to judge the success of a group by the relations between persons.
   ——— (c) I am usually pretty quiet in groups.
   ——— (d) I think a group should discuss a project thoroughly before it acts.

3. Family
   ——— (a) Families need to make decisions together.
   ——— (b) Family members should not interfere in each other's life.
   ——— (c) Parents should have firm control of family life.
   ——— (d) The best family is one in which everybody has fun.

4. Job
   ——— (a) Individuals should do their jobs and not worry about other people.
   ——— (b) People who work together ought to enjoy each other.
   ——— (c) The job goes better if one person directs it.
   ——— (d) Persons who work together should make decisions by consensus.

5. Recreation
   ——— (a) Recreation that involves a number of people is more satisfactory.
   ——— (b) Recreation ought to be a part of a general health plan.
   ——— (c) I prefer recreation that is done alone (reading, jogging, etc.).
   ——— (d) Recreation plans should be negotiated with others.

6. Travel
—— (a) Travel is a way to get away from daily routine.
—— (b) Travel is a good opportunity for learning.
—— (c) The planning is about as much fun as the trip itself.
—— (d) I enjoy going on trips because of the people I meet.

7. Leisure
—— (a) I have a regular hobby or activity on which I like to spend much of my leisure time.
—— (b) I prefer to spend leisure time by myself.
—— (c) Usually I enjoy spending leisure time in places where there are a lot of people.
—— (d) I often make plans with others for using leisure time.

8. Conversation
—— (a) When the conversation lags, I try to provide a topic to keep it going.
—— (b) I like animated conversations with a number of people.
—— (c) I try to listen carefully before responding to other people's statements.
—— (d) I often find it difficult to get into a conversation.

9. Issues
—— (a) Things would work out better if people would leave well enough alone.
—— (b) One ought to hear all sides of an issue before making a decision.
—— (c) It's more important to have friends than to win arguments.
—— (d) Some things you just have to take a stand on.

10. Temperament
—— (a) Whenever possible, I avoid hurting people's feelings, even if I feel frustrated.
—— (b) I get annoyed when people can't see the obvious facts in the situation.
—— (c) I think living requires a lot of give and take.
—— (d) If people want my opinion, they will ask me for it.

11. Decisions
—— (a) When I make decisions, I often wonder whether people will approve.
—— (b) It's so hard to make decisions that I sometimes put it off for a long time.

——— (c) I usually get another opinion or two before I reach my conclusion.

——— (d) I feel that I usually reach decisions fairly quickly.

12. Initiative

——— (a) Mostly, I wait for group consensus before acting.

——— (b) My style is to think a while alone before I act on new information.

——— (c) I work best when people are around.

——— (d) You could probably describe me as a self-starter.

Scoring

Write numbers for each section beside appropriate letters below.

		Purpose	Passive	Participative	Person
1.	Life Plan	(c) _____	(d) _____	(b) _____	(a) _____
2.	Groups	(a) _____	(c) _____	(d) _____	(b) _____
3.	Family	(c) _____	(b) _____	(a) _____	(d) _____
4.	Job	(c) _____	(a) _____	(d) _____	(b) _____
5.	Recreation	(b) _____	(c) _____	(d) _____	(a) _____
6.	Travel	(b) _____	(a) _____	(c) _____	(d) _____
7.	Leisure	(a) _____	(b) _____	(d) _____	(c) _____
8.	Conversation	(a) _____	(d) _____	(c) _____	(b) _____
9.	Issues	(d) _____	(a) _____	(b) _____	(c) _____
10.	Temperament	(b) _____	(d) _____	(c) _____	(a) _____
11.	Decisions	(d) _____	(b) _____	(c) _____	(a) _____
12.	Initiative	(d) _____	(b) _____	(a) _____	(c) _____

TOTAL _____ _____ _____ _____

_____ _____ _____ _____

Personal Tendencies and Leadership Styles
Descriptions of Leadership Characteristics

The tendencies assessed in the accompanying test often affect the style of leadership employed by an individual. Some ways in which persons may function in group situations are listed under each style. Remember, each person may have only some characteristics of a preferred style and the combination of tendencies may change the ways any function is actually practiced. All styles are useful in appropriate circumstances. Each person probably has some of each.

FIRST: Make a bar graph of each style using the space provided.

SECOND: Read the descriptions of your dominant styles and compare them with your behavior in leadership roles.

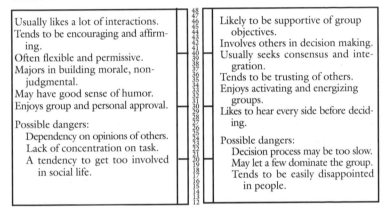

PERSON

Usually likes a lot of interactions.
Tends to be encouraging and affirming.
Often flexible and permissive.
Majors in building morale, nonjudgmental.
May have good sense of humor.
Enjoys group and personal approval.

Possible dangers:
Dependency on opinions of others.
Lack of concentration on task.
A tendency to get too involved in social life.

PARTICIPATIVE

Likely to be supportive of group objectives.
Involves others in decision making.
Usually seeks consensus and integration.
Tends to be trusting of others.
Enjoys activating and energizing groups.
Likes to hear every side before deciding.

Possible dangers:
Decision process may be too slow.
May let a few dominate the group.
Tends to be easily disappointed in people.

PASSIVE

Offer group autonomy and freedom.
Values predictability and order.
Probably very loyal to the group.
Often good at resourcing and referencing.
May consider many possibilities before acting.
Encourages harmony and calmness.

Possible dangers:
Sometimes fails to participate in process.
May procrastinate.
At times blames others for errors.

PURPOSE

Typically provides firm leadership in groups.
Usually good at delegating and coordinating.
Acts decisively and maintains direction.
Responds well to challenge and opportunity.
May direct activities and persons effectively.
Highly focused and enduring.

Possible dangers:
Sometimes tends to judge others severely.
Lack of flexibility in time of stress.
Can become autocratic with others.
Occasionally feels martyred.

The Cathedral Option

This instrument title is from the story of the manual worker who said he was building a cathedral.

A) Have persons fill out the form on page 94 with the appropriate numbers and transfer the numbers to the totals at the bottom.

These will be used later.

B) Delegate someone to collect and average the numbers for the whole staff for each item (i.e., #1, average 3.7). Share the results.

C) Note the highest and lowest averages. Ask the members to state why they think that these are high or low. If there are no numbers lower than 4.3 ask why they think they are so high. (Any number under 2.5, however, is cause for further examination.)

D) Then ask staff persons to give their own totals for the scores at the bottom of the page, along with any comments they may have.

Competency means the level of perceived skill on the job.

Affirmation means the level of approval from others.

Significance is a measure of how important persons feel they are in the overall operation.

E) If there are low scores for the group or for individuals begin immediately to devise plans for improvement. Follow up.

Staff Models Inventory

This is an adaptation of an instrument developed by the American Lutheran Church.

A) Have each person fill out the form (pp. 96-97) in advance of the meeting or retreat (note the different scoring pattern) and transfer the numbers to the columns provided.

B) Have someone add the totals of the columns and average them for the group.

C) In the session explain that the column titles refer to how staff responsibilities are determined:

Structural: by the way the church organization works (certain committees/boards require it that way)

The Cathedral Option
An Instrument for Measuring Personal Satisfaction

Place a number in blank: "5" if nearly always true
"4" if usually true   "3" if moderately true
"2" if occasionally true   "1" if seldom true

1. I do my job well. _____
2. Other staff members think I am competent. _____
3. What I do is important to my constituencies. _____
4. I enjoy being asked to provide help. _____
5. My work expresses my faith. _____
6. I feel affirmed by fellow staff members. _____
7. What I do is essential to our purpose. _____
8. I am comfortable leading groups. _____
9. I am sure that I was chosen for my ability. _____
10. Other staff persons help me when I need it. _____
11. I am included in staff decision making. _____
12. My constituencies express appreciation. _____
13. Other staff persons accept me as I am. _____
14. My work is important to me. _____
15. My skills in the job are growing. _____
16. The director approves of my work. _____
17. I feel excited about what I am learning. _____
18. My work here will contribute to my career. _____

Place the Numbers in the Appropriate Blanks Below:

Competency	Affirmation	Significance
1. _____	4. _____	3. _____
2. _____	6. _____	5. _____
8. _____	10. _____	7. _____
9. _____	12. _____	11. _____
15. _____	13. _____	14. _____
17. _____	16. _____	18. _____

TOTALS   _____   _____   _____

Custodial: by custom and/or facilities
(established practice or a demanding plant, etc.)
Linear: by the administrator (senior pastor or other)
Relational: by consensus of the staff itself
D) Determine which model the staff has voted to be the dominant one, second, third, and fourth. Ask the staff members if they feel that this actually describes the way they work. Also ask if they feel this is the way it ought to be. If not, how do they change it? If so, how do they convey their approval to the personnel committee or church? Develop a strategy in either case.

E) Finally, ask persons to discuss whether their individual numbers agreed with the averages. If not, why not? What are the reasons we view staff models differently?

Vision Supersedes Supervision

There is much talk about vision these days, in both religious and secular organizations. Clearly no institution gains momentum unless there is a vision of the future. Some claim that the pastor is the one who originates the vision for the congregation so that if he or she has no vision there is none. Our theology of the gifts can hardly agree with that. Vision, like any other Christian construct, may come from anyone who is seeking the will of God. However, there is a need for someone to gather the scattered parts of the vision and put them together for the body. The pastor may be the one to do that, but only if he or she sets time aside to ponder the aspirations of the people and the will of God and find a way to collate and correlate them into a whole vision for the church's future ministry. The staff team can be an integral part of that process and build itself up as it participates. Everybody's vision involves everybody.

It must be said that great insight often serves the cause of Christ more than good personnel management skills. *Vision*

Staff Models Inventory

For each statement in this section you are requested to indicate which of the four responses most accurately reflects your perception and feelings about your staff. You will have ten points to distribute over the four choices, but no one item may receive less than one. The higher the number of points assigned to a response, the more completely that response corresponds to your perceptions or feelings.

The following are example combinations:
A<u>7</u> B<u>1</u> C<u>1</u> D<u>1</u> or A<u>4</u> B<u>3</u> C<u>2</u> D<u>1</u> but not: A<u>8</u> B<u>0</u> C<u>1</u> D<u>1</u>

(1) Goals for ministry are:

___A. Established by leader

___B. Decided by the whole staff

___C. Established by job descriptions

___D. Largely set by circumstances

(2) Authority:

___A. Is primarily a function of position

___B. Derives from the organization

___C. Depends on constituents' approval

___D. Is held by the whole group

(3) Jobs are usually:

___A. Assigned to individuals by the leader

___B. Assigned by job descriptions

___C. Assigned to individuals by the staff

___D. Determined by program and plant

(4) Agenda of staff meetings:

___A. Are developed by the staff

___B. Are usually routine

___C. Are determined by staff leader

___D. Are set by program/facility needs

(5) Staff decisions about ministry are made:

___A. By leader

___B. In consultation with constituents

___C. By group consensus

___D. Through organizational expectations

(6) Members usually see themselves as:

___A. Sharing a relationship

___B. Protectors of special interests

___C. Advisors to the leader

___D. Participants in a common cause

(7) Church programming tends to emphasize:

___A. Cooperation between staff members

___B. Staff responsibilities to committees

___C. The leader's goals and priorities

___D. Performance of assignments

(8) The way the staff functions:

___A. Is a responsibility of the leader

___B. Is generally taken for granted

___C. Is examined and discussed by staff

___D. Is less important than duties

(9) Feedback on individual performance:

___A. Comes from church members

___B. Is given by staff members

___C. Is given by the leader

___D. Is rarely given

(10) The staff spends most of its energy:

___A. Being a model Christian community

___B. Helping the leader do his/her ministry

___C. Helping individuals do their own ministries

___D. Helping the whole team do its ministry

Scoring

Transfer your score from each item to the chart below, then add the columns to obtain your index for each model.

Structural	Custodial	Lineal	Relational
1. C ___	D ___	A ___	B ___
2. B ___	C ___	A ___	D ___
3. B ___	D ___	A ___	C ___
4. B ___	D ___	C ___	A ___
5. D ___	B ___	A ___	C ___
6. D ___	B ___	C ___	A ___
7. D ___	B ___	C ___	A ___
8. B ___	D ___	A ___	C ___
9. D ___	A ___	C ___	B ___
10. A ___	C ___	B ___	D ___

TOTALS:

[___]   [___]   [___]   [___]

Team Spirituality: A Guide for Staff and Church by William J. Carter. Copyright © 1997 by Abingdon Press. Reprinted by permission.

supersedes supervision. Persons caught up in a dream for the future may become self-directing and highly focused. Less supervision is required because the goal is clear and compelling. The staff that participates in the visioning process may discover its own identity and ministry and become a more effective team, but all need to understand that discerning the vision is not simple.

Vision cannot be fabricated. It cannot be thought up on demand, or manufactured from petty aims, or packaged to fit some preassumed personal goals. It does not happen every time we want it to, and it often comes from unexpected sources. (One of the characters on the television sitcom "Mad About You" declared that he was a "peripheral visionary." That could be what it sometimes takes.)

True vision emerges from the environment. Seldom can we bring vision with us. What worked in the last parish may have little relevance to the present. Pastor, staff, and even members who bring their old church expectations with them may have to reassess their assumptions. A knowledge of the community and a search for the will of God for the present situation is vital each time. Leaders in the visioning process are first listeners and learners. "They are great synthesizers, masters of selecting, synthesizing and articulating an appropriate vision of the future" (Harris W. Lee, *Effective Church Leadership* [Minneapolis: Augsburg, 1989], p. 135).

Vision does not happen every day. It comes in the fullness of time. Years may pass before a defining vision emerges in any situation. (In a seminar on vision in Nashville, I asked three hundred pastors to recall the last time they felt their churches were motivated by a great vision. Almost all named a time far in the past.) More than one pastor and staff may have to wrestle with it. If we are to be effective we must anticipate future vision at the same time that we are doing ministry based on past vision. One of the most interesting insights into the early church is Paul's struggle in accepting the leadership of Apollos as recorded in the first letter to the church at Corinth.

Apollos was a new paradigm preacher (see Acts 18:24-25) and the people of Corinth were delighted with him. Paul feared that they were losing themselves in their excitement over this great orator. But as he writes he sees a great truth. Ministry is not about who is the most approved at a given time, or who is most loved. It is about sequences and stages. "What then is Apollos? What is Paul? Servants through whom you came to believe, as the Lord assigned to each. I planted, Apollos watered, but God gave the growth" (1 Cor. 3:5-6).

The fulfillment of the dream may await the unexpected interpreter, a good thing to remember when we begin to take credit for some surge of growth or vitality. Who knows how many servants of God it takes to reach the foundation stones of ministry? It will certainly take the whole staff at any given time and place.

Vision is doomed without a strategy for its fulfillment. Vision undergoes clarification and strengthens as it is subjected to the critical light of practical application. Time for planning is important to all ministry, but nowhere is that more true than in the implementation of vision. Both staff and people should be a part of the strategy.

It may be a waiting game, but it is worth the wait. Vision changes things. Everything! But it may take more than one leader to see it through. Understanding the vision of our predecessors and preparing for the vision of our successors are primary tasks of the ministry. The gospel is forever. We are transient (the United Methodists call it itinerant), but the church will endure to the end of time. Vision occurred before your arrival and will be occurring after you leave. If each person insists on his or her unique vision, the life of the church will consist of chaotic episodes of activity alternating with years of the doldrums. (Or at least it has so far.) Understanding and claiming the vision of others may be the best way to begin a process that will lead to new vision.

Administration through the gifts requires that leaders

spend time in envisioning, planning, and consulting with people and staff. This "processing" time is not wasted. It may be the most fruitful use of all. As we wait in prayerful anticipation for the voice of God, the voice of the people, the cry of human need, and the harmonizing insight we are genuinely participating in the ministry of God's Body.

Becoming the Local Church Renewal Team

The assumption of the traditional staff structure is that staff persons are chosen for particular areas of ministry (youth, evangelism, financial management, education, senior adults) and that they are expected to improve that ministry, approaching perfection. But there are two limits to perfectibility: (1) Perfection is constantly being redefined—the target moves as we move toward it, and (2) even when we have reached perfection we may find that it is not what was needed after all. In the light of these limitations it is possible to see that another description of staff may be preferable.

A contemporary definition of staff function is that *the staff exists to ensure that the body will always be renewing itself in the spirit and image of Jesus Christ, its head.* That also happens to be a biblical image. Our charge is "to equip the saints for the work of ministry, for building up the body of Christ, until all of us come to the unity of the faith and of the knowledge of the Son of God, to maturity, to the measure of the full stature of Christ" (Eph. 4:12-13). Programs and emphases are in constant flux, but the goal is forever fixed: It is to bring the body to be more like Jesus in every way.

There is substantial literature that insists that revitalization is impossible anywhere without a complete redesign of the *entire* system. I believe there is too much evidence to the contrary to allow that theory to go unchallenged. The current guru of systems thinking has a succinct word to say about that: "Systems thinking also shows that small, well focused actions can sometimes produce significant, enduring improvements, if they are in the right place" (Peter M. Senge, *The Fifth Discipline, The Art and Practice of the Learning Organization* [New York: Doubleday, 1990], p. 64). Churches are systems, but the whole system may be changed when any vital part is energized, and the inability to reorder the whole body is no excuse for failing to revitalize body parts, one congregation at a time. It is not always possible to predict which part will provide the entry point for new life. We may have to try a few before we discover the significant ones, and when we are most unaware we may find the key. Local church staffs individually and corporately become the catalysts for renewal in the parts or in the whole body.

Church staffs who are given the opportunity, the support, and the freedom to experiment with ministries and to see their ministries in the context of the whole ministry of the body can affect the life of a church very deeply. And that, along with laity who are also unleashed, respected, and supported, can bring renewal to a congregation, even if they have to do it within the constrictions of community, denominational, and regional or national protocol. In fact, if there is no renewal, as some claim, within the old parameters, then most of us, like a majority of the overweight, are doomed to eternal frustration.

The laity, pastor, and staff of a local church are the renewal team, and the only one, that can resurrect its spirituality and redirect its energies. Whatever renewal happens will have to be within the physical, mental, and spiritual capabilities of that team, assisted by the power and presence of Christ in the midst. And it will happen where they are, not in a distant parish, or from a denominational headquarters, or out of a book, or through following someone else's prescription. Both the process and the accomplishment will build the staff team into a stronger, more unified crew.

The center of the renewal matrix is the vision and gifts of the members of the body. Some individuals or groups are

always longing for a path to a closer walk with God. Someone, somewhere in the local church is constantly voicing a
complaint, a suggestion, or a hope. Every church is awash
with ideas when ears are attuned. The current local paradigm
often does prevent us from taking these comments seriously.
The tiniest threat of criticism is countered by the shield of
paradigm protection. "Oh, we can't do that." "Our church
has never done that." "Our denomination doesn't approve of
that." (The lines are from my own mouth at various times.)
Sometimes that is true, and once in a while we do need to discourage harebrained schemes, but more often it is a pretext
for inaction. Our desire for security in our positions becomes
stronger than the power of God in us for renewal. It is as
often the pastor and staff who resist the forces of change
(which may lead to renewal) as it is the members of the
church. Most of us, too, have egos and turf to protect and
axes to grind. And, of course, when the church is at a stand-
still, with the staff champing at the bit, there is always the
danger that some members of the church who have a great
emotional investment in the way things are will reject any suggestion for change that may come from pastor or staff, even
though it may have great promise for the revitalization of the
body, or some part of it. Their chief interest is in protecting
customs and patterns that have become comfort zones, and
are therefore precious in their sight. What can we do to open
the possibilities for revitalization?

Roles of the Staff Team in Setting a Climate for Change

The foundation role of the staff in renewal for the congregation is in its responsibility for discovering and deploying
the gifts of the members of the body (of which they are part)
until the whole body reflects its head. How can the staff, as a
team, help set the climate for change?
The first role is that of teacher, which may take awhile

(remember that Barnabas and Paul taught the people for a whole year). The whole staff must be *engaged in continual education of the congregation on the biblical foundation and theology of the gifts, and on listening for the call of God on their lives and for the church.* This is a new paradigm—one that we are already living with.

There are three principles of gifts discovery that need constant repetition:

1. We do not always know why God calls those whom he calls. In spiritual innovation members of the old paradigm do not always recognize paradigm pioneers, or the meaning of God's call.

2. God sometimes equips us after he calls us. He does not just call the obviously equipped. There are times when we confuse skills and gifts, believing that we and others will always be called to do what we do best. But gifts are more comprehensive than skills, and not so easy to define, or pigeonhole.

3. The gifts and the appropriate time and place must be united before persons gain fulfillment in gifts deployment.

Staff members teach others how to test the call by being willing to submit their own to the scrutiny of the body, as well as Scripture and pragmatic criteria. We do not help persons to understand the reality of the call by insisting that ours are always genuine and theirs usually suspect.

A second role is *to practice and promote transformational ministry.* That term has become a cliche in many quarters, perhaps because it is overused by workshop leaders to mean some mysterious quality of leadership possessed mainly by the speaker. But there is nothing mysterious about it. It simply means that leadership should be directed toward the goal of changing (transforming) the participants and their setting to enable them to become their vision of themselves. The first transformation may have to be in the leader, who must be willing to be changed along with his or her constituency.

Change is systemic. Every part of the system is transformed as any is changed. Those who model participative decision making and flexible leadership styles promote transformation of the whole body.

The primary task of the transformational team is to arouse confidence that persons can actually reach their objectives and accomplish their goals. Speed Leas says, "A transformational leader is influential in strengthening and inspiring followers rather than trading with or overpowering [them]" (Speed Leas, *Leadership and Conflict* [Nashville: Abingdon, 1982], p. 32). Transformational leaders provide a rousing sense of buoyancy and assurance. They carry the group along with them toward the vision: persuading, adjusting, and redirecting until the aim is reached. The staff team must embody this attitude and encourage it in others.

Good leadership springs from spiritual energy and Christian attitudes rather than forceful personality traits. The dynamic can become the demonic without genuine commitment to Christ, the head. Pastors or staff persons who stubbornly insist on their own way or jealously guard their professional domains tell the congregation that such behavior is acceptable. So laity are likely to behave that way, too. When staff and pastor are willing to listen, respond, and adjust to the opinions and suggestions of others, and to participate with them in trying new ministries and methodologies, there is a far greater likelihood they will accept a proposed fundamental change and participate in it enthusiastically.

Two of the central themes of Total Quality Management are that "barriers between staff areas must be eliminated" (and, I might add, the barriers between staff and congregation) and that "fear of authority must be driven out." The whole group becomes a resource for discovering areas for improvement and empowerment anywhere. Surely the Body of Christ can reflect that motif as well.

In the third place, the staff must *generate a process for staff understanding and consent in the development of its own ministries.* In too many cases there is little communication between staff persons on program matters and no unity of direction or purpose among staff members themselves, which virtually eliminates any successful revisioning process.

The fourth role of the team is to *help the church become a learning organization.* The church, like any other vital body, must be "an organization that is continually expanding its capacity to create its future" (Senge, *The Fifth Discipline* [New York: Doubleday, 1990], p. 7). The church has always been an institution devoted to learning, but that may be quite different from being a learning organization. Devotion to learning can be a device for preserving the past, while true learning is the process of "continually" creating the future. The pastor and staff will be the central factor in that learning process.

The mastery of leadership is not in knowing the organization and serving it, but in the commitment to "the discipline of continually clarifying and deepening our personal vision, of focusing our energies, of developing patience, and of seeing reality objectively. As such it is the cornerstone of the learning organization—the learning organization's spiritual foundation. An organization's commitment to and capacity for learning can be no greater than that of its members" (Ibid., p. 14).

The staff team demonstrates its own commitment to being a learning organization by doffing the mantle of theological and professional presuppositions with which it arrived and opening itself to the guidance of the Spirit and local insight in discerning the vision and ministry that represents God's will for the congregation. The people join in the learning process as they abandon their accustomed patterns and look for the new vision that will reunite them in the renewal of God's power in their midst.

CHAPTER FIVE

Experiencing Spirituality

The Staff Growing Toward Its Core Ministry

For most of the twentieth century we have been saying that local church ministry must focus on spiritual growth—but it has often been difficult for the traditional churches to define and address that conviction. The theme is being expressed even more frequently today. Engendering spirituality is the core of our ministry together and the first duty of all who work with the people of the church.

For emerging churches, as we all once were, spirituality becomes the practice of the *dominant theme* of the new body, and being Christian is defined as participating in that process. In many such cases persons who do not practice the dominant theme are not considered Christian, even though they may have most other characteristics of a biblical or traditional faith.

For the enduring churches spiritual growth is not so easy to define. Many generations have added their definitions (or confusions) to the mix. So the search may take many forms. For some persons spirituality may be defined in terms of daily private times of prayer and devotion, for others by an intense involvement in some special setting—such as a retreat. Some will seek the practicality of acts of compassion or discipleship, others may desire an expression of the reality of God in personal and community relationships. But, however defined, *the common expectation persons have in a local body of Christ is*

106

that they will discover new resources of faith, that their spiritual lives will be enriched. Even the communions that stress the once-in-a-lifetime experience that makes us Christian instantly and forever ("once in grace, always in grace") still lay heavy emphasis on prayer, doing the work of the Lord, and becoming better equipped to respond to God's call.

There is a desire for faith development—spiritual growth — in every congregation, and in most persons. Any activity of the church that responds to that need is judged to be more spiritual than any activity that addresses more "physical" needs. Even though the New Testament does not seem to draw a line between physical and spiritual in defining discipleship and readiness for union with God, the common feeling is that the inner person must be awakened to the reality of God before the activities of the Christian community become productive.

The Spirituality of Vocation

The senior pastor and staff will benefit from attention to this expectation, and be evaluated on their achievement of its implied goals. The most common expression of approval of any staff person is that he or she helps persons to be or feel more spiritual, and the most widespread criticism is that pastor or staff or both are not spiritual enough.

> After being away from one of my former pastorates for ten years I was invited back to preach a New Life Mission. It was a happy time and I felt free to really cut loose in the pulpit. Toward the end of the week an elderly woman who had been a great friend, supporter, and sometime critic during my years as pastor said, "Well, Bill, the whole time you were here I kept praying you would get religion and I think you finally have."

> After the laughter I thought about that a lot.
> Although I do not really think my commitment was any
> deeper the second time around, my way of expressing it
> had changed. I used the Bible more, had developed a
> more personal presentation style, and used illustrations
> that had "inspirational" impact rather than thesis sup-
> port. Furthermore, I was more relaxed and could be
> warm and communicative rather than grimly deter-
> mined to set them straight. Come to think of it, I may
> have gotten a little religion. In any case it met with the
> approval of my friends. They like for us to show some
> "spirituality."

It follows that attention to faith development (especially in its perceived spiritual dimension) becomes a primary function of staff, as well as a primary need of persons who are on staffs. Because the spiritual needs and expectations of persons are as varied as the gifts, and may be closely related to them, the process of response to need may take many forms. Whether these needs emerge within the staff or from the congregation they are at the core of our ministry and deserve our full attention.

There is no exclusive requirement that church staffs be involved in spiritual search and growth. That is a part of the development of every whole person. But the church staff ought to be an example for others of the integration of spiri-tuality and vocation. A member of one staff that I adminis-tered reported to a "popcorn" session (real popcorn) one morning how surprised she was that a call to a local business had resulted in a recorded message that the staff was having its quiet time in preparation for the day and suggested that callers leave a number. She said, "That insurance company was having a quiet time and here we are crunching popcorn. Shouldn't we be more like that?" While we finally decided that fellowship was more important for us than solitude on the job, and that we did have our quiet times too, the discussion was helpful to us all. We concluded that spirituality was for everyone, but that each group has to select modes appropriate to its own needs.

Individual persons who are members of a staff will have certain spiritual needs which must be met in order to make a more fully effective performance of ministry possible. (Our model here may be the apostles in their life with Jesus. They too grew in knowledge and devotion as they worked together.) In many cases these needs are met through private devotions, personal acts of piety, and discipleship experiences, which build up the inner life. But, while most individual needs will ultimately have to be met in individual ways, it is the responsibility of the staff administrator, and each staff person, to be open to and supportive of spiritual development efforts of fellow staff members.

The Imperative for Spirituality

The staff will come to an understanding of its spiritual growth needs as a body and incorporate processes that assist the journey to wholeness in its everyday group life. The routine use of Bible reading, prayer, and devotional time may be all that some staff want from the common times together (and some may not even feel a need for that), but there are often underlying tensions and feelings of deprivation that can be relaxed by some attention to spirituality. Beyond that there are arenas of personal and corporate growth that may develop from a focus on spirituality that do not occur when there is too much reliance solely on skills training and group dynamics. And finally the staff will want to be familiar with various spiritual search models in order to increase the potential for responding to their own emerging needs and those of the congregation.

The most common complaint from pastors is that there is just not enough time in the busy week of the congregation for the staff to engage in spiritual search and discovery. There are so many things to do and so many programs to resource that staff meeting time has to be held to a minimum, and cannot be used up on hour-long exercises, meditation and prayer, and interpersonal conversation. That may be true, but if it is, it may indicate some problems with both church and staff:

1. It may say that the church itself has been taught that activities are more important than spirituality. If we must resource five basketball games and host ten community events and manage the social life for fifteen fellowship groups, administer the Sunday school and other learning groups, arrange and conduct worship services, attend twenty committee planning sessions a month, maintain liaison with the youth groups, women's groups, and men's groups, oversee the use of twenty-five classrooms and thirty self-help, physical fitness, and luncheon sessions, then it is possible that we do not have time. It is also possible that we have run amok with programming and need to reassess the priorities of the body, as well as the staff.

2. If the church, the senior pastor, or the staff feels that none of these events can take place without one of them being present *we have already lost faith in the grace of giftedness.* The whole congregation is an extended staff and should be assuming responsibility for its own programming and spiritual enrichment. In this case what is good for the church is good for its people.

It takes far less time in the long run to discover and equip leadership for each new activity as it emerges and set it free to make whatever contribution it can to the life of the body. If it does not succeed it can be supplanted by another ministry with more promise and newly equipped leaders. The staff's role in the discernment and preparation of persons to do ministries has its payoff in the way it frees staff to pursue its own spiritual development and lead the church to greater spirituality. This, of course, may mean that the more it succeeds the less the old staff roles may be needed, and the more staff persons will be forced to refocus gifts or give way to others with new skills and gifts that fit the new dimensions of the life of the body.

3. Even if the transformation in the life of the church does not happen rapidly, and it probably will not, the staff still has its own spiritual needs to fulfill. We have berated clergy for many years about the emptiness of their own spiritual lives (in a library full of books and thousands of workshop topics), and we cannot afford to allow the staff to fall into that same ecclesiological trap: That is *we cannot substitute managing the body for being the Body.*

4. At least one of the responsibilities of the staff is to serve as a role model for spiritual development. Unless the members of the body see the staff involved in the search for spiritual meaning they may not value it themselves. The apostles took time apart with Jesus more than once. Prayer, meeting human need, fellowship meals, and lessons on spirituality were part of their life together.

All of this adds up to the conclusion that not only can we afford time for the most central activity of Christian persons, but we cannot afford to neglect it. Spiritual growth is a fundamental part of the life of the staff.

Resourcing One Another

One of the first tasks the staff sets for itself may well be to discover what level of *corporate devotional activity* is most comfortable for the entire group. That may vary from a prayer to start a weekly staff meeting, to a regular meditation time for all staff in separate rooms, to a daily devotional time with hymns, prayers, and verbal or interactive "inspirational" content. (Staff administrators who like the idea of a religious pep talk every day may need to check with the staff to be sure that pepping up is what they feel the need for.) I have developed a very simple instrument to use as a discussion guide:

Devotional/Spiritual-life Survey for Staff

Rank each of the following items by putting "3" beside the statement in each numbered section that best expresses your feeling, "2" beside the next choice, and "1" beside the one least representative of the way you feel.

1. a. As a staff we ought to have daily devotions. ___
   b. The quality of relationships is more important spiritually than frequent group devotionals. ___
   c. Devotions at staff meetings are enough. Persons should have their own personal devotions ___

2. a. I value personal spiritual support from staff ___
   b. Staff devotions give me spiritual strength. ___
   c. I have a personal devotional life that is sufficient for my needs. ___

3. a. Individual prayer is better then public piety. ___
   b. The best expression of spirituality is the way we relate to our constituencies. ___
   c. We have too little group spiritual expression. ___

Add the numbers for the following lines:

Corporate	Relational	Private
1a. ___	1b. ___	1c. ___
2b. ___	2a. ___	2c. ___
3c. ___	3b. ___	3a. ___

TOTALS ___   ___   ___

Team Spirituality: A Guide for Staff and Church by William J. Carter. Copyright © 1997 by Abingdon Press. Reprinted by permission.

Those who have a higher score on "corporate" prefer group spiritual expression, those in the "relational" column feel that interpersonal expressions are the most meaningful, and those who have a higher score on "private" value personal devotions (the New Testament closet model) the most. (In some cases scores may be very close together in all columns, which indicates either a broad view of spiritual potential or a wishy-washy personality. Take your choice.) Similarities and differences can provide fruitful discussions. Interpretations are up to the staff members.

The very process of negotiating the amount of group life to be given to overt religious expression may become an opportunity for persons to examine the meaning of spirituality and the relationship of external exercises to the vitality of the inner life. If allowed to proceed freely these discussions could be the beginning of some creative approaches to corporate spiritual expression. When appropriate the nature of these discussions, and the resulting pattern or discipline, may be shared with the congregation. They will not only be comforted to know that the staff is thinking about spiritual growth and the devotional life (they often fear that the staff is not so inclined), but some may be encouraged to examine these issues with family, friends, and groups.

Exercises for Sharing Spiritual Experience

Resourcing one another may mean *sharing spiritual insights from life experiences* as a part of or in addition to other group devotional moments. The role of intimacy in the development of groups is widely discussed these days. For the church staff there is no more useful arena of intimacy than the personal knowledge of one another's faith pilgrimages. However, some persons have dramatic stories to tell (and others have a flair for the dramatic), that can intimidate

those with more commonplace experiences. I have found it
useful to develop some group exercises that enable persons to
begin to share in nonthreatening ways. They may be helpful
in starting the staff toward an examination of its spiritual
understanding and resources.

One is a simple design from my book *Each One a Minister*
(Nashville: Discipleship Resources, 1987, pp. 18, 19) called
the "P-Square." I have used it with staffs and many other
small groups. Persons are asked to draw a box and divide it
into four parts, and fill in each part with a:

❏ **Person** who has influenced your spiritual journey
❏ **Place** important to your spiritual growth
❏ **Period** when your spiritual journey took a new direction
❏ **Passion** (concern) that has absorbed you at some time.

PERSON	PLACE
PERIOD	PASSION

Then ask persons to share with the others any category
they choose, with a brief explanation of the effect on their
spiritual development. If there is time, take another turn,
sharing a different category. Be careful not to force. Let anyone pass. After all who wish to do so have shared, ask: How
did that make you feel? What do we know about one another
that we did not know before? What is influencing your spirituality now? Close with prayer.

Another exercise comes from experiences in small groups:
In advance of the meeting ask persons to choose one Scripture passage of no more than ten verses that they feel is most
important to their spiritual understanding. In the meeting

have each person write chapter and verse or verses on newsprint or chalkboard and read the scripture without comment. After all have read ask each one to complete this sentence, in writing, using no more than thirty words: "The scripture I chose is important to my spiritual life because _____." (For instance, one might read the "love your neighbor as yourself" passage and complete the sentence by writing, "It gives me a single standard by which to judge my relationships with other people.") Pass these around, and let each person read all the written statements. Open the discussion for comments and questions. If desired, repeat the exercise a few weeks later with other scriptures.

The most complex of these exercises is one I call the "Spiritual-life Dimensions Survey." It uses a variation of John Westerhoff's typology of stages in spiritual experience as a framework for a survey instrument that can be used to open discussion of differing spiritual dimensions among persons.

Provide each person with the survey and ask each to complete it and add the scores before the staff meeting or retreat. (See the survey form on pp. 116-17.)

1. Have each person complete the form and add the scores before the meeting or retreat.

The *experiential* dimension measures the level of commitment to a personal view of faith, with a major emphasis on inner assurance, verbal expressiveness, and interpersonal witness.

The *affiliative* dimension is an indicator of commitment to a corporate faith expression, with major emphasis on being members of the Body of Christ, the activities of the institutional church, and familial relationships.

Searching indicates the strength of the desire for theological or operational changes, which could range from social activism to charismatic expression to organizational restructure.

Spiritual-life Dimensions Survey

(Put #4 beside first choice in each section, #3 beside second, etc.)

1. Worship
___ a. Worship is most effective when it stirs people emotionally.
___ b. Worship is best when I enjoy God with people I know and value.
___ c. Real worship challenges people to change the way they serve God.
___ d. Worship is supposed to prepare persons for service outside the church.

2. Sunday School
___ a. Sunday school classes should confront people with faith issues.
___ b. Sunday school classes succeed best when they make people feel included.
___ c. A worthwhile project is important to the success of a class.
___ d. Sunday school should help people grow spiritually.

3. Personal Spiritual Growth
___ a. Spiritual growth is most likely to occur in a group of caring persons.
___ b. True spirituality is most often found outside the traditional church.
___ c. The test of spirituality is the willingness to become a servant of humankind.
___ d. The best plan is just to turn everything over to the Lord.

4. Property
___ a. Church property should be used to serve the needs of the community.
___ b. The church building ought to be a place where Christians enjoy spiritual fellowship together.
___ c. The church building ought to be respected and cared for.
___ d. The church needs to quit worrying about property and start being the church in the world.

5. Christian Community

___ a. The Christian community are those searching for a true faith.

___ b. Christian community is wherever people are doing ministry.

___ c. Those who have confessed Jesus Christ as Lord are the Christian community.

___ d. The basic Christian community are those who are part of the church fellowship.

6. Outreach

___ a. The mission of the church is to bring people to Christ through evangelism.

___ b. We need unconventional forms of mission to reach the people who need it most.

___ c. The best form of outreach is through the church, supported by its members.

___ d. Christians need to be personally involved in outreach ministries.

Scoring

(Transfer numbers to blanks below, then total.)

Experiential	Affiliative	Searching	Missional
1a ___	1b ___	1c ___	1d ___
2d ___	2b ___	2a ___	2c ___
3d ___	3a ___	3b ___	3c ___
4b ___	4c ___	4d ___	4a ___
5c ___	5d ___	5a ___	5b ___
6a ___	6c ___	6b ___	6d ___
___	___	___	___

Team Spirituality: A Guide for Staff and Church by William J. Carter. Copyright © 1997 by Abingdon Press. Reprinted by permission.

Missional dimensions are those which indicate objectives beyond the local church, in community and world.

2. Point out that all dimensions are part of a whole body, but that most individuals have a dominant one at any given time. They may change over time or as a result of experiences.

3. Ask persons to identify the dimension on which they scored highest (or those tied for highest) and give a brief (two minutes or less) explanation of why they feel that dimension came out first on their forms.

4. Have the group discuss how these dimensions complement one another, and how each enriches the whole team. Point out that these same differences exist in the congregation and that they make it richer, too. They are part of the variety Paul approves.

The number of such exercises is legion. The Serendipity Workshops of a decade ago made them popular and many resources are still available. Constant repetition of similar experiences can become boring and unproductive, but a few planned exercises as the group goes through its inclusion stage can open doors for constructive interchanges later on.

Adjustments Outward

Just as beliefs differ from community to community and church to church, so do behaviors. Sometimes the staff projects a confusing wrong image of its spirituality to those in the community because its customs are different. While the inner motivation may be excellent, the outward signs are not consistent with the expectations of persons in the church. An exercise in defining and understanding these differences might be helpful.

At one of its gatherings the staff could discuss the difference among themselves and between themselves and the congregation in the way they work in public. In some cases the staff may be more demonstrative of spiritual convictions than the leaders of the congregation and give the impression of self-righteousness. In other cases they may be less demonstrative and leave an impression of spiritual paucity. Making a list of ways they differ from the congregation is a good starting point.

When the list has been completed the staff might discuss these questions: (A) Which of these differences are the result of differing convictions, and which are simply habits? (B) What can the staff do to change its public behavior without losing its self-respect? (C) Will the effort at change actually bridge some of the gaps?

For instance, one inhibited staff had these ideas for adapting to a much more demonstrative congregational mode:

1. We need to reveal our own prayer life more (pray for congregation, request their prayers).
2. We should make a special effort to be with "spiritual groups" that meet in our church.
3. We will openly use Scripture, carry a Bible.
4. We will use more "spiritual" terminology.
5. We will let people know we are searching for a deeper spiritual understanding.

Adapting to the habits of others in the congregation ought to recommend itself as much as adapting to the customs in a new country. Wherever we are our spiritual expression will be more convincing if we make its terms familiar to the people.

Becoming a Support Group

The staff as a whole, like any other body of Christ, can *become a support and recovery group*. As persons experience life they will probably experience pain. Sometimes the pain of life can interfere with both competence and spirituality. At such times the staff can become a resource instead of an added burden if it can bring to focus its common concern and spiritual energy. While intercessory prayers are a staple of Christian groups, there is more that may be done by those who are prepared.

A helpful preparation for such times of crisis might be the planned use of staff meeting time (or a short retreat session) to learn together some of the characteristics of support and recovery groups. A member of the staff or someone from the community can provide leadership. The rudiments of listening skills, empathetic response procedures, and the dynamics of support and recovery can be learned from a book, a psychiatric nurse, or a local counselor. But the real value is in the process. As we learn together (become a "learning organization") we mature as an instrument of God's will and as a resource for congregational needs. The added benefit is knowing that when our time comes to suffer "the slings and arrows of outrageous fortune" the staff will help us to carry on through the time of distress.

The symptoms of spiritual deprivation and confusion may take many forms: in behaviors that produce alienation, or expressions of dismay and pessimism in inappropriate settings, or more direct questions about faith and loss of personal awareness of God. Staff members can be of great assistance to one another by simply providing a sympathetic ear, demonstrating openness, and showing support. Sometimes it is even possible to enter a spiritual mentoring relationship, but care should be observed to avoid imposing on others our own solutions to their problems. Unless staff persons sustain one another in personal and faith crises there is little hope that they can find other areas of common ministry.

Discovering the Means of Grace

Since the primary focus of the ministry of the church is faith development, and the growth of the spiritual life, the staff could profitably spend some time in the discussion of the means of grace and the practice of disciplines that encourage spiritual growth. Norman Shawchuck and Roger Heuser say that "the extent one is willing and able to weave the spiritual delights, or the means of grace, into one's own private life will determine one's ability to minister effectively" (*Leading the Congregation* [Nashville: Abingdon Press, 1993], p. 42). They speak of the three elements of the spirituality of Jesus: (1) He carried out his ministry within the context of a small, intimate, covenantal community (sounds a little like a staff, doesn't it?); (2) he established a rhythm of public ministry and private time; and (3) he taught by example that the six "graces"—prayer, fasting, the Lord's Supper, the Scriptures, spiritual conversation, and public worship—were vital to life and ministry (Ibid., pp. 46-48). Surely the staff will find these helpful in finding a starting point for their own examination of group spirituality. More than an afternoon could be spent profitably in group discussion about the meaning and value of these means of grace.

For many persons the most valued part of the spiritual relationship is prayer. There are more books on prayer than any other religious subject, and so many methods are suggested and different results sought that they may be a source of confusion instead of help. Nor can a whole prayer life be found solely within the confines of staff function. But the staff can and must be in prayer. Without it there is little hope of success in either ministry or personal spiritual fulfillment. Beyond that, staff can also be involved in learning to pray, as a discipline and as a personal resource. Prayer can be both an experience and a learning methodology.

One possibility for a guided study is the use of a book such as *Celebration of Discipline* by Richard J. Foster (revised ed. [San Francisco: Harper, 1988]). Divided into three sections: The Inward Disciplines, The Outward Disciplines, and the Corporate Disciplines, the book examines the spiritual life thoroughly and with great insight. Twelve topics are pursued including prayer, study, service, confession, and celebration. One-hour sessions over three to six weeks, along with private study and meditation, could be instrumental in the development of a deeper understanding of what spiritual disciplines are all about.

Because of the nature of the gifts (we all are different because God needs different persons and personalities to do all the work of God) we must be careful not to expect everyone to benefit from the same interactions and experiences, including staff persons. Those who work for the church need to be growing in faith and spirit as much as those who are recipients of the ministry they bring. Periods set aside from time to time for the examination of the spiritual life of the group, and some new goals or redirection, are appropriate, and vital. The sharing of concepts, experiences, and processes among staff persons can lead to exciting insights. Times of spiritual introspection and reflection, in staff meetings or in retreat settings, can be crucial to the growth of the ministry of the staff.

Broadening the Base of Spirituality

The staff may also benefit from opportunities to *examine the concept and practice of spiritual growth, formation, and renewal with someone from outside the group.* Since spiritual formation is very popular these days, there are many itinerant practitioners. A retreat or staff meeting devoted to one of these models, led by a person with experience and expertise (nearby, for just the local staff, or with other groups in a setting beyond the parish), can be the catalyst for deeper examination of personal and group life. While any model itself may not appeal to every staff person, an exposure to a number of them leads to insights that are valuable to all. In addition to which the very act of being together in a time not devoted to the tasks of administration and programming can be both invigorating and renewing.

In a retreat I led a judicatory staff composed of ten people through some team-building activities and a brief review of their interpersonal relationships. In discussing the ways in which the group had changed the most in the last year, one of the support staff spoke up to say that she felt much closer to other members of the staff than she had a year earlier. I asked her why. She said it was the result of some sessions on spirituality led by a former staff member. In the discovery of the deeper meaning of the spiritual life she had come to love and value her fellow workers more.

As members of staff come to grips with their own spirituality and see the ways in which others have approached spiritual growth, they will broaden the base of their own spiritual search, and ultimately of their own relationship to God and one another.

Staff Covenants

Perhaps more important than any other aspect is that staff relationships are not merely among persons who happen to work for the church. They include a pact with God. The response to the call to ministry and the formation of a work team that helps persons find a more satisfactory relationship with God and with other human beings clearly implies a covenantal relationship. It is this *covenant*—between each person and God and between each person and all the other persons involved in the ministry—that forms the bond that binds the staff to one another and to the body they serve. Without this covenant all is vanity. *Until persons are committed to a corporate ministry that originates in the will of God and culminates in the justification and perfection of Christian disciples there is no ministry, there is only labor.* (Of course we are using the Wesleyan meaning of perfection, which implies a constant search, but does not assume total achievement.)

Although many groups can function without a written covenant, it is always assumed a covenant exists. Putting it in writing may be beneficial to everyone.

The development of a covenant can be a supremely spiritual endeavor. As persons attempt to state their perception of God's call on their lives, the giftedness which accompanies the call, and the way those calls fit together in a local ministry, as well as what they can expect of one another in regard to performance of ministry, it is possible for spiritual perception to be deepened, for bonds to grow stronger among persons, and for the vision of God's will to take on new vitality and urgency. The formation of such a covenant, and its constant redefinition and renewal, is the power driver of staff life. Not only when new staff members join, or new visions emerge, but regularly and deliberately the staff should review and renew its covenantal relationship in order to reflect its highest perception of God's will, and the very best performance of ministry in the Body of Christ in which they are called to employ their gifts.

Elements of Covenants

A covenant should include *a statement of faith*. That is different from a statement of beliefs, a distinction that should be respected. Faith is a condition of acceptance, a willingness to trust God and the transforming power of God's grace as experienced through Jesus Christ. Simple statements are best. If specific personal or doctrinal interpretations are included, make sure that they are essential to the purpose of the group. For example, a statement of faith: "We commit ourselves to follow the Lord and seek God's will for our lives." A statement of belief is more creedal: "We believe in the holy catholic church, the communion of saints . . ."

There should be some *definition of ministry:* what persons feel ministry to be and where its standards originate. There might be references to the call, the will of God, and the purpose and mission of the staff or congregation, and to conditions that define ministry as vocation.

The document could briefly outline *expectations of one another,* especially matters such as respect, ethics, and support for spiritual needs and ministry functions. *Decision-making* procedures are important. The proportion of direction from the staff administrator, dependence on job descriptions, staff consensus, and custodial tasks (see Staff Models Inventory, pp. 96-97) should be discussed and a statement made. General policies about the initiation of new ministries and relationships with congregational planning bodies might be included.

Time and responsibility levels are a good subject for covenants. When persons are expected to be together, at what time the workday starts and expectations for hours and evaluation can be included.

Other elements may be important to some staffs and not to others. Remember, it is your covenant! If, however, you wish to share it with your personnel committee, or even the congregation, it might give evidence of your commitment.

Here is a sample covenant:

As persons who feel they are called of God to serve the body, we express our confidence in the providence of Almighty God and give thanks for our individual experiences of justification through Jesus Christ. We commit ourselves to follow God's lead and to constantly seek his will for our lives.

We feel that ministry is of God and that it is expressed through the gifts he has provided us and the whole Body of Christ. We covenant to allow our gifts their highest expression and to seek to discover and implement the gifts of the people.

We expect of one another respect for opinions, loving support in times of stress, and an adherence to the highest standards of moral and ethical behavior, and will always observe complete confidentiality in our relationships with one another. Suspected breaches of these standards will be discussed with the staff member privately, with an effort to resolve issues, but employment continuity may be affected by any of them if they threaten the ministry of the body or the unity of the staff.

As representatives of the body we will, insofar as we are able, carry out the mandates given us by the body for the employment of our selves, our time, and our talents, while always seeking the call of God to better ways and higher skills.

We will be prompt in time commitments, diligent at work, and open to adjustments that may be necessary to fulfill the expectations of the people of the church through their experience of God's call and commission. Decisions about the use of our time and the focus of our ministries will be made in the light of the stated mission of the church, with the assistance and advice of our senior pastor, and in consultation with one another at weekly staff meetings and other times of community.

As personnel change and the life of the group matures the nature of the covenantal relationship may also change. Once done, the written covenant is more of a reference point than a rule or canon. It is subject to constant refinement and revision to meet the challenge of new insights, new vision, and new responsibilities. At least once a year, or every time a person leaves or joins the staff, it is a reasonable goal to examine the covenant for reconsideration.

Journaling and Other Private Times

Group activities will not be the best expression of spiritual search for everyone. In place of, or in addition to these more verbal and interactive processes some will feel the need for quiet reflection and personal meditation. To the "religious" (monks and nuns) of the Middle Ages such devotions seemed essential. Hours, days, and weeks were spent in disciplines which included study of the Scriptures, prayers, fasting, and silent retreats. In our time the rediscovery of these spiritual formation procedures has spawned a variety of books, worship aids, retreat centers, and societies for spiritual discipline. Becoming acquainted with the best of these will allow staff persons whose spiritual search is more inwardly directed to develop proficiency in the exploration of inner spiritual reality.

In her book *Journaling, A Spirit Journey* (Nashville: The Upper Room, 1988), Anne Broyles outlines six possible areas of life in which reflection and recording may be helpful: (1) in the events of daily life; (2) in response to Scripture; (3) with guided meditations; (4) after dreams; (5) in response to reading devotional materials; and (6) in remembering conversations. She remarks that "putting one's life down on paper is often helpful as a clarifying process" (p. 13). Since God is active in the world, and a part of every step we take, every breath we breathe, there is great merit in taking time to discover the meaning in the salient moments of life and writing them down for future reference and reflection. For instance, there are conversations that dwell in our souls. Allowing ourselves the time to capture the essence of that exchange and finding words to express it can intensify and lengthen the effect.

Instead of abandoning our inner life to a stream of consciousness that leads only to meandering circles of self-serving themes, we can direct some part of our existence to the inspection of the geography of the soul surrounded by God. From these experiences we can gain strength for the stress of piercing the boundaries of life with a ministry of the word. And "we can integrate reason and imagination, what is proven and what is unknown, our conscious and our subconscious thoughts. . . . On this journey we can come in touch with the God who is at all levels of our consciousness" (Ibid., p. 62).

Here, as elsewhere, there is a great emphasis on prayer, but this is prayer that springs from the desire to know God, not that which comes from the desire to use the power of God for some other purpose. Seeking the power to intercede for others, or to win converts, or to effect desirable changes in the human condition belongs in the realm of legitimate ministry, but nothing can replace the prayer that is uttered only in the presence of the Most High and asks only that we be God's, and God be ours.

Even for those who derive great satisfaction from spiritual experiences that are primarily focused on interactions and activities, the reminder of the value of the inner life is relevant and cautionary. There is a very thin incorporeal membrane between the inner and the outer life, and those who concentrate on the outer tend to toughen the shell inside of which their most secret self resides. But it is that self that must be open to God, not merely the one displayed for consumption by those whom we serve. Not just those staff persons who already seek an inward path, but every person who is in ministry can benefit from time spent discerning the presence and will of God.

Henri Nouwen reminds us that we cannot minister out of nothingness:

> Ministry and spirituality never can be separated. Ministry is not an eight-to-five job but primarily a way of life which is for others to see and understand so that liberation becomes a reality. . . . It must be possible to find the seeds of this new spirituality right in the center of Christian service. Prayer is not a preparation for work but an indispensable condition for effective ministry. Prayer is life; prayer and ministry are the same and can never be divorced. (Henri J. M. Nouwen, *Creative Ministry* [Garden City, N.Y.: Doubleday, 1971], p. iii)

The development of the link between the inner life and the life of service cannot be neglected by those who seek to become purveyors of the gospel message in word and action. The pastor and staff would do well to provide assistance and encouragement to those who want and need to pursue the inner life.

One to Get Ready, Two to Go

We cannot completely equate spirituality and effectiveness in ministry. When we do we tend to destroy some of the substance of each. Spirituality is the resource of life. It belongs in the realm of basic existence. We cannot live without it. Effectiveness in ministry is a more practical matter. Experiencing spirituality may or may not make us more popular as ministers. Some are effective in some areas with little apparent spiritual intensity. Innate skill or knowledge can sometimes carry the day, and persons may be made aware of great spiritual truth even by those who do not reflect it themselves. We all know persons who are loved, respected, and followed in spite of our certain knowledge that they have feet of clay. But there is more.

The exploration of spirituality is not just for the enhancement of ministry, although it will surely achieve that. It is fundamentally for the union of humanity and the divine. Persons who know God are more able than persons who do not—but their ability is in the realm of the spirit and not the flesh. It is a marvelous thing when spirituality and proficiency are united, but the primary focus must be on spirituality. It is much easier for a spiritual person to gain proficiency than for a merely skilled person to gain spirituality.

So, staff persons are seeking the presence of God together because it is the route to wholeness and harmony, internal and external. If in that process they discover some ways of helping others to spirituality it will be a double blessing. In our next chapter we will look more closely at methodologies for assisting in the exploration of spiritual insights by persons in the congregation, and for helping the whole congregation to a more lively expression of spirituality.

CHAPTER SIX

Mediating Spirituality

The Core of Ministry

The pastor and staff of a church that has been in the same slow-growing community for decades are faced with a dilemma that does not occur among those whose primary role is "planting" new churches. The church planters usually move into a promising area and start a church configured for those who are dissatisfied with the settled churches or have no church at all. When things work out they are able to set the agendas and select the worship styles and choose a governing board and staff to complement their ministry. While many do not succeed, there are a large number of such churches these days. When they do not succeed, they move to another area (if so called) and do it all over again.

But staffs in enduring local churches (denominational or community) must acknowledge the presence of a few hundred, or a few thousand, persons whose spiritual life has been nurtured for a lifetime through a style of worship, fellowship, and ministry that they or their parents helped build. For many of those persons the loss of the environment in which their spirituality flourished and waned and flourished again is devastating (as it sometimes is to those nurtured in the independent church environment when they join a traditional church). The worship setting, sermon style, and musical genre sustain and satisfy. The programmatic offerings provide not only a place to be in fellowship and learning with others but also a source of pride in community circles, where the youth program, the singles ministry, the annual Christmas pageant, or even the Christian Dieters' Club attracts coverage from the local newspaper.

In most enduring churches there are periods of time when there is discontent and loss of spiritual vigor. Occasionally the dissatisfaction burgeons into rebellion, and a new pastor, staff member, or other leadership regime is inaugurated. Sometimes it just goes on year after year, gnawing at the fabric of the life of the church. The problem may be the pastor or staff or both, persistent critics, an ineffective governing board, a congregation with the wrong values, or almost anything the human mind can consider annoying. Whatever the cause, a revival of spirituality is the objective.

We have already said in the foregoing chapter the primary focus of the congregation is to help persons grow spiritually and to deploy them in settings that enable them to express it in meaningful ways. That will differ from church to church because God calls each of us, as persons and bodies, to use our individual gifts in ways that build the body toward its head, Jesus Christ. Even as we have different gifts to offer we have different needs to satisfy. It would be foolish and enervating to start a new church to fill each spiritual need (though some have tried). The New Testament keeps reminding us that the same body can encompass a great variety of gifts, and is even strengthened by them, so it is surely able to address a variety of spiritual needs, and derive strength from that, too. Investigating the spiritual needs of enduring congregations, and what will satisfy those needs, is a major focus of ministry in these churches and therefore a primary task of the staff.

A Place for the Staff to Start

In consultations with congregational staffs we have often engaged in an exercise designed to help the staff examine its relationship to the spirituality of the body. It begins with a request that the staff define its own understanding of spirituality by listing on newsprint or chalkboard words and phrases that describe what *spirituality* means to them. Such metaphorical phrases as "closeness with God," "love for others," or "living for Jesus" may be mentioned. After ten to fifteen items have been offered, the list is collated, and staff persons are asked to draft a statement of what spirituality means to them, including as many of the ideas as practical. (The process may take an hour or more.)

The staff is then asked to define what spirituality means to the congregation in the same way: with words and phrases. After the list has been completed they are asked to devise a paragraph that gives a summary definition of spirituality for the congregation. After all have agreed on a statement the two views of spirituality are compared to see how closely they coordinate with each other. Differences and similarities are recorded. (This will take another hour or so. Time should be scheduled to enable completion of both parts of the exercise in one or two sessions.)

Some discussion is initiated about ways of bringing the views of spirituality closer together. How can the staff become more like the congregational definition of spirituality, and how can the staff help the congregation to embody more of the staff's description? Some staffs come up with an excellent list of possibilities (which takes another hour or more). Often there is some willingness to adapt to congregational expectations.

However, someone may say, sooner or later, that the description the staff gives of the congregation's understanding of spirituality may or may not actually reflect the real views of the people. (If nobody says that, then the leader should.) After spending considerable time talking about what we think spirituality means to them (and revealing our own presumptions), it may be wise to engage the congregation in an examination of its own views of what facilitates spiritual development in the body. Since there are both many different needs and many different expressions, to achieve optimum spiritual impact it is necessary to discover the meaning and practice that will enable the present congregation to rediscover basic directions for spiritual growth and expression.

Helping the Congregation Define Its Spiritual Needs

There are two aspects of congregational analysis regarding spirituality. One has to do with *the dynamics of spirituality:* the meaning of the spiritual life to the participant. The other focuses on *the components of spiritual expression,* which deals with the elements of group life that promote spirituality. For some persons the dynamics may be all important (how to feel close to God, the meaning of prayer); for others the focus is on patterns of congregational life (worship styles, small groups); while others may consider missional activities the best foundation for spirituality. Views about each of these are important in developing responses to spiritual hunger.

Helping the Congregation Define Spirituality

Helping the body define spirituality can be a source of growth to staff and members. We are so accustomed to spending our time setting goals for building campaigns, testing designs for new programs (even spirituality programs), and managing public relations that we lose sight of the reason for it all (or, at least, what should be the reason). Discovering what persons consider to be spiritual has not been a high priority. We just assume that what we routinely do should provide spiritual support because that is what we have always routinely done and nobody that mattered has complained.

One way of engaging the body in a spiritual search is to ask each unit to reach a definition of "spirituality" and share it with the others. If the church is already divided into small geographic groups, they would be the logical place to start. But if not, then ask every Sunday school class, the men's groups, the women's groups, the youth groups, other age-level groups, each program committee and ministry area, and any other small groups that may be active to spend one or more meetings discussing the meaning of spirituality. (A helpful preparation would be to call together one leader from each group for a brief period of instruction on the process.) From that meeting would come a description of the meaning of spirituality for each group. These might be printed in the newsletter or a special bulletin, perhaps a few at a time over several weeks.

Have a task force made up of staff, class or group leaders, and others, prepare a summary statement, including the main ways in which spirituality is described. Here is a paraphrased statement from one church:

When thirty-four groups in our church were asked to prepare statements on "What Does It Mean to Be Spiritual?" everyone responded. Statements varied from a paragraph to two pages in length and focused on many topics. As the local church Task Force on Spirituality we have prepared the following summary to serve as a guide for our spiritual growth ministry. We believe that these five items represent the main ways in which we describe the spiritual life:

1. Spirituality is an attitude about God that puts God first in our lives. It means loving God with all our heart.

2. Being spiritual means acting in ways that show that God is present in our lives. It involves both acts of compassion and moral living.

3. Spirituality is the cultivation of the inner life of meditation and prayer. It is the ability to be with God and listen to God.

4. Spiritual living is listening to the Holy Spirit. It is being open to the guidance of the Spirit as we make decisions and do ministry.

5. The center of the spiritual life is Jesus Christ. Being spiritual is sharing Jesus with people.

We believe that these five areas of Christian living are common to us all, and we propose to order the life of the church so as to stress these spheres of spiritual growth. We solicit responses from the members of the church regarding this statement.

In another, newer church with a different focus and history, the groups who were asked to define spirituality almost all said the same thing. The summary provided for the church was brief and centered on a few concepts. Here is their statement:

As members of the congregation we have examined all the statements from the classes and groups in our church and have prepared the following summary for use as a basis for our ministry together.

We believe that spirituality is defined as the work of the Holy Spirit and that the entire membership should be directed toward hearing, through prayer and self-discipline, the word that the spirit gives to us. As we experience the spirit's presence we will find power for healing, witnessing, and daily living.

Clearly the last statement will require a different response from the first. The staff and representative persons from the congregation will want to develop processes that meet expressed needs in each situation.

Discovering Preferred Spiritual Growth Environments

A second approach to developing a helpful environment is to *discover what types of activities are considered most conducive to spiritual growth by those who are expected to benefit from them.* As with the definition of spirituality, there is a difference among persons in what they consider valuable for spiritual growth. If we know what activities are most likely to be beneficial we can emphasize them in planning and implementation.

One way of addressing the matter is to develop a survey instrument. They serve three purposes:

☐ They focus the congregation on the subject.
☐ They affirm that personal opinions are important.
☐ They give program planners data instead of guesses.

The judicious use of instruments is an excellent way of establishing communication between the church people and the staff and other leaders. I have used the following survey with congregations in a number of settings to enable leaders to assess the spiritual resources that congregational members value most. Like all instruments this one should be adapted to the needs of the local body.

The number of persons ranking any item high may vary greatly from church to church. Groups of people differ measurably in choosing among spiritual growth options. The church that develops its spiritual life emphasis in response to these needs will soon experience a marked improvement in the feeling of spiritual satisfaction among the people.

This survey can be scored by volunteers, and should be. Participation by members of the congregation enhances the experience. First sort by the category at the bottom. Each team of two can count forty to fifty forms. Numbers for each item should be added together and divided by the number of survey forms to get an average ranking. In that way it is possible to see what types of practices provide the most assistance to persons in their spiritual search, and even to compare members with visitors. Information should be shared with the congregation. Where indicated, groups may be formed to initiate ministries or improve those already in existence.

A Suggested Procedure

When the data has been analyzed, the staff and others can respond with accuracy. If the highest numbers are on items 1,

Where I Find Spiritual Resources

Put a *number* beside each of the following items that indicates how helpful that activity is in your spiritual growth (1. Not helpful, 2. Slightly helpful, 3. Beneficial, 4. Very helpful):

1. Private meditation and prayer ____

2. The church worship services ____

3. Solitary Bible or spiritual growth study ____

4. Helping others meet their needs ____

5. Small-group Bible or spiritual growth study ____

6. Listening to inspirational TV/radio/tapes ____

7. Following a disciplined program of devotions ____

8. Retreats at secluded places with good leaders ____

9. The right kind of music (worship or other) ____

10. Special preaching services (revival/renewal) ____

11. Going on a short-term mission trip ____

12. Spiritual support groups with other searchers ____

13. Working in community service agencies ____

Check: Member___, Attend reg.___, Leader/teacher___, Visitor___

Comments:

_____

3, 6, and 7, emphasis should be placed on developing resources for personal devotions. If the highest numbers are on items 2, 9, and 10, then attention might be given to emphasizing worship. High numbers on 4, 11, and 13 show a desire for service activities, and on 5, 8, and 12 the use of intensive spiritual growth groups. Here are some possible actions:

Personal devotions: provide printed guides and materials; suggest prayer chains and intercessions; have tapes and other resources in the church library;

Celebration: seek further definition of elements; develop worship styles that meet needs; refine and improve music choice;

Service/mission: develop community projects; relate to outside mission groups; create a personal service process

Growth groups: obtain resources materials; encourage group formation; provide training for leaders

Various combinations can be interpreted to help develop a profile of activities that will involve those interested in spiritual growth in processes they find helpful. *Allotting time for the exploration and improvement of the spiritual growth environment of the church can be life-changing for both staff and congregation.*

Each of these methods involves the whole church in examination and discussion of spirituality. If the staff and other leaders elect to follow such a course it should be with careful planning and absolute concentration. No competing churchwide activities should be allowed to distract persons from their focus on spiritual meanings, yearnings, and processes. Only the staff can ensure that program time is cleared. Three or four weeks devoted to a consideration of spiritual values and exercises is time well spent. Other things can be done at other times.

Encouraging Spiritual Growth Through Congregational Life

Staff persons should broaden their spiritual horizons by building personal knowledge and skills for leading persons of all ages in the search for faith development and spiritual growth all the time. Because the spiritual needs of persons in the congregation are even more varied than for those on the staff (there are so many more of them), a crucial part of the preparation of staff persons (yes, including the support staff: those who provide typing, cleaning, bookkeeping, and other services) for ministry will be to discover more and more ways in which spirituality may be encouraged and strengthened among the people of God, through staff involvement.

Helping others to a mature spirituality is not easy. Like trust building within the staff, it does not happen by convening a meeting about "spirituality in our church." It certainly does not always mean the involvement of persons in a packaged spiritual life program on the assumption that they will emerge fully prepared for abundant living. The very nature of the giftedness of each person, which God has set as God wished, means that each has a different path to preparedness and different criteria for fulfillment. Spiritual growth will involve different approaches as persons mature. Both package and presentation will have to be changed at intervals in order to help persons move toward God.

The senior pastor and staff are not necessarily spiritual growth experts (although some may have a special gift for helping persons in spiritual development), but they should be able to mediate access and resources through which persons can grow. That means that staff persons should be sensitive to spiritual needs, familiar with resources, and willing and able to accompany persons on whatever journey would seem to be most advantageous to the person and the time, in whole church settings, small group sessions, study classes, and in individual relationships. Faith development and spiritual growth are a product of the interaction of seekers, leaders, and the Holy Spirit of God in every department of the church.

This emphasis on spirituality is not intended to encourage persons to become Pharisees for Christ. The terms *faith development, spiritual growth,* and *spirituality* are used in a complementary way (they are not interchangeable, but overlap), each carrying a slightly different meaning but all conveying the breadth of the search for the presence of God. One of the enemies of the search is pompous piety, that form of religious behavior that exaggerates the goodness of one person at the expense of others. Blatant expressions of sanctimony and covert displays of self-righteousness can do more harm than good, because they manipulate others to admire the actor instead of the God whose presence is being invoked. To be hoped is that growth can be anticipated as much in the one who leads as in those who are learning. Staff and congregational leaders who mediate spiritual growth opportunities successfully will always remember that God has the same care for the inept as for the professional, for those who stumble as much as for those who stride confidently ahead. Biblically, it is the poor in spirit, those who are not so sure of themselves, who may well lead the way on the final leg of the spiritual journey.

Mediating Spirituality Through Worship

The mediation of spirituality may take place through the worship of the church, where every staff person is crucial. Spirituality may be more affected by the details than we imagine. The atmosphere of celebration is greatly affected by music, so leaders and accompanists make a difference. The printed order of worship matters, so secretaries make a difference. The comfort of the sanctuary matters, so maintenance persons make a difference. There is even a move afoot to engage coordinators of worship (paid or volunteer) who take care of the details. Every staff person may have an effect on the acceptability of the worship experience. Nor must we overlook the volunteers: ushers, greeters, worship coordinators, altar guilds. They too influence the atmosphere in the sanctuary or auditorium.

A church in the Atlanta area was instituting a new worship service, for a total of three different ones each Sunday morning. What surprised me was that they had hired a professional service to train their ushers. One staff person had been assigned to supervise the process during and after the training, but the value of these volunteers was enhanced by the attention to their skills.

Whatever else it does, the center of the life of the congregation is its weekly Sunday gatherings. Scripture, prayer, music, and sermon may together become a powerful spiritual resource—if those structuring the service carefully plan elements that respond to the needs of persons where they are. Too many musicians choose music to meet music school criteria rather than congregational spiritual needs. Too many preachers go for the razzmatazz instead of the warming of hearts. Too few laypersons are visible leaders of worship. The worship, especially on Sunday morning, should be the most exciting and spiritually satisfying time of the week.

The Celebration Service

For a growing number of churches, the central source of spiritual vitality is their services of "celebration," derived from the great Protestant tabernacle services of the nineteenth century. The first of these may have been the African Methodist Church in Charleston, South Carolina, pastored by Morris Brown in 1817. Lively music, inspirational preaching, and evangelistic fervor marked this church of about

3,000 members (which grew in spite of laws against the gathering of slaves for any purpose). Other churches took up the format and by the first part of the twentieth century there were many.

For these churches the central core of spiritual growth was the weekly gatherings, usually Sundays and Thursdays, where persons were thrilled by the music, heard the Word, and responded with commitment. (One of my older mentors once called that type of church service a "spiritual refreshment center.") Great preaching by a gifted orator was the most visible characteristic, but staff also was of great importance. Directors of music were essential, and such leaders as Homer Rodeheaver became famous. Pastoral care was done by a staff of clergy who visited the sick and counseled those who sought to know the Lord. Sunday school directors, such as Louis Entzminger in Dallas, who built up the largest Sunday school in the world at that time, with an average of 5,200 in attendance, became as famous as the pastors.

(Staff developments in these churches affected staff organization in all churches. For most of the early twentieth century, staff was composed of secretaries for the pastor, clergy for pastoral care, and laity [with a few clergy] as leaders of music and education. Only recently has staff configuration begun to reflect changing emphases in local church ministries and a predominance of laity.)

For a number of years the tabernacle worship pattern was a great influence on some Protestant churches, but in the fifties and sixties a strong liturgical revival restored orders of worship based on Protestant versions of medieval church liturgies. These "standard" orders of worship are considered normal today in many traditional churches, and everything else is for special occasions, but many young people and some adults (who remember the tabernacle services with nostalgia) long for something else. In many congregations the most often mentioned complaint is that the worship services are boring. The service has little excitement or enthusiasm, few extemporaneous elements, and no movement.

Celebration services usually open with sprightly music accompanied by a variety of instruments, followed by enthusiastic singing of old favorites and newer hymns and choruses. Hymnals are seldom used. People know the songs or the words are "lined out" by the leader, or projected on a screen. Printed orders of worship are rare. Everything is informal. Persons are encouraged to be active. In some churches prayer times are offered at the altar with many participants. Intercession is made for the troubled, and praise offered for victories. Sermons are straightforwardly based on relevant human needs, and most services close with a call to spiritual renewal. There is great variety; not all follow the same format, but most include many of these elements.

Ironically, when local leaders come together for conferences and conventions, they are often involved in celebration-type services, and derive great enjoyment from them, but do not see them as possibilities for their own churches. They are viewed as "entertainments" rather than true worship. Walt Kallestad's or William Easum's declaration that effective evangelistic worship must include entertainment arouses considerable resistance in many traditional pastors, and in church members as well. I have experienced that myself:

After three years at Brainerd United Methodist Church in Chattanooga, Tennessee, we had a highly dedicated and creative staff. God had given us a Christian educator, an associate pastor, a business manager, and a director of music who were extraordinarily able, and very flexible, along with an excellent support staff. We decided to get with it.

Wednesday evening was our first venture. Pushed by a group of older laity who wanted a midweek Bible study, we turned it into a spiritual learning experience and fellowship for all ages—Bible study from kindergarten to senior citizens, along with some optional sessions for those who had other topics to explore. And, of course, we had a fellowship supper. Attendance mushroomed.

Then we decided to affect the morning worship. The music director organized a jazz group, a country music group, a brass ensemble, and a rock group, one of which performed about once a month. We started singing "gospel hymns" and choruses in addition to the standard hymns. We had a children's sermon and leaders who helped them sing happy anthems for worship. I left off the robe except for Communion Sundays. We began having laity read the Scripture and offer the morning prayer. When I preached my associate sat in the congregation, as I did when he preached. We had dialogue sermons and role play, drama and skits.

It was fun, and it involved people, but not everyone. A few left to find places where they could have the old-style worship. Some stayed and fussed. Most enjoyed the traditional services and the once-a-month celebrative events equally. Many said their spiritual lives were enriched. New persons came and stayed. After a while it just seemed as if we had always done it that way.

But investigating or dabbling in this sort of renewal is no longer an option. The mood of the world has changed. For a high percentage of younger persons

- ❑ Spirituality is defined by excitement rather than serenity.
- ❑ Music is energizing rather than soothing.
- ❑ Oratory is rhetorical rather than logical or analytical.
- ❑ Mass activity rather than solitude defines the environment for life-changing decisions.

So, it is no wonder that an increasing number of commentators on the religious scene are saying that worship elements need to be enlivened in order to meet the spiritual needs of these younger members of our culture, and many older ones. My experience in the past few years, and particularly in the past few months, supports the idea that a more stimulating worship style dramatically changes the spiritual climate of the service, of the staff, and of the whole church.

I have attended many such services. They vary in effectiveness in proportion to the skill of the leaders and the mood of the church, but in every case three shifts are apparent: (1) The audiences are markedly younger; (2) participation is more intense; and (3) many persons are present who have not been attending church at all, or recently. In most services the level of expressed spiritual enthusiasm is higher both in and out of the sanctuary, and the church is also growing in attendance and membership. Just as the eighteenth-century tabernacle movement, with its emphasis on contemporary music and personal decision, led to bigger and more enthusiastic crowds, so the late-twentieth-century celebration, with its contemporary music and high emphasis on *emotive* spirituality, reaches a new audience.

An important consideration in planning any innovation is whether it will change some essential element of belief or heritage for the worshiping congregation. I am convinced that the environment enlivens the event, but that the content may be varied to confirm the convictions of the worshipers. The songs chosen, the texts used for preaching, and the comments made by leaders are where persons get their clues concerning the tenets of faith. To maintain our momentum as Christian witnesses in the local church and community, we may have to adopt the styles of others in order to gain the power to communicate our ancient content.

If the decision is made by pastor or staff and people to introduce a celebrative style (and, after experiencing it in many places, I do recommend that it be tried), either as a replacement for the ones now used or in addition to them, staff support and spirituality become pivotal. In order to introduce a worship style that will excite, energize, and change the level of spirituality for persons, it is absolutely essential that the entire staff related to worship be both skilled in the details and harmonious in the generalities. A poorly done traditional service is boring. A poorly done contemporary service is embarrassing. Almost equally important is that all other staff be supportive and encouraging. A time of innovation is not the time for debate on merits among staff. Issues should be resolved long before "C-day."

Music is central to celebration. Musicians will have to be reoriented, retrained, supplemented by others with the right skills, or replaced, in order to get the proper feel and content. Not everyone can play a spirited tune on the piano, or lead the congregational singing with panache, or develop the sequence of a song service gracefully. Not everyone even wants to. Persons without familiarity with new Christian music and the gospel songs of yesteryear will need to learn them or give way to those who are or will. William Easum claims that the traditional music was a deliberate device to discourage universal participation: "The Euro-centric stodginess that surrounds so much of the classical [music] scene was perpetuated since the Reformation in order to keep out the riffraff" (*Dancing with Dinosaurs* [Nashville: Abingdon Press, 1993], p. 90). The simpler melodies and snappier tunes for biblical and Christian concepts are where the future lies. Here are some steps to include celebrations in your church:

1. *Develop familiarity.* For some persons spiritual resources have always come from the traditional liturgy. They will need to see convincing evidence that another approach will provide the same values, or be assured that the style that sustains them will continue to be available. Elements of the celebrative experience can be illustrated from time to time in tradi-

tional worship and used on special occasions. Only the best should be shown, and it should be clear that no persons will be forced to accept a format they find inappropriate for their own spiritual growth.

2. *Gain consent.* Many of the independent churches have small governing boards (five or six persons), which can quickly come to a decision. Most denominational churches have much larger boards, and committees galore. If the staff is to remain in good favor and the congregation is to become receptive, there must be a careful shepherding of change processes through appropriate bodies with skillful communication with the congregation.

3. *Begin as an experiment.* Some avid proponents advise quick and radical change, justified by the good results that can be expected later. But nearly every one of them reports initial conflict and defections. The question is, "Just how much disruption of existing spiritual environments, which satisfy many, is justified in order to install a new one for others?" After all, who are we to say that existing spiritual content is inadequate just because it does not meet our expectations? Our gifts paradigm allows for many expressions of spirituality, even declares that they are desirable because it was God who made us all different *by design*. It may be that "different strokes for different folks" is a profoundly theological statement.

Finding an appropriate time and place to experiment with the celebration service and offering it as an option for those in the body, and an enticement to those outside, seems to be a reasonable compromise. Perhaps one of the multiple morning services, or a Sunday evening, or even a Saturday evening (now being tried in a number of communities), would be a good place to begin. It may mean having more staff, but that is a small price to pay. Fundamental change can be disruptive. What is a little time and staff salary if it brings harmony to the body? Let people see. Let them learn at their own pace. Let the Spirit lead them. Let the youth lead them. It may be that there will be two or three permanent contrasting services, but many already have multiple services. Why not see if one of them can serve a different audience—as an experiment?

4. *Gather a staff.* The crux of the matter is the staff because the staff will experience and model a different depth in its own spirituality as it mediates the Spirit through a celebrative form of worship. Again, the key is the pastor. Unless he or she has confidence in the objectives and is comfortable with the process, it should not be undertaken. But, once underway, the staff takes center stage. Musicians must be enthusiastic, co-celebrants must be focused, and everyone must demonstrate a sense of spiritual confidence (but not arrogance) and an awareness of audience needs. Nothing works unless the staff (some of whom may be full-time, part-time, or volunteer) provides the skills and momentum to bring it off.

All staff may, and should, participate in the service. Visibility here will show solidarity and express confidence in the staff. Some may be asked to help train ushers, counselors, and children's church leaders. (As time goes on all these should be the responsibility of the laity, but in the beginning staff may have to do it.) The support staff will need to be especially aware of promotional responsibilities and the preparation of the sanctuary. There is something for everybody to do in creating a successful celebration experience.

5. *Constantly evaluate and improve.* This step is a must. While the innovation is in the development stage every staff person and some congregational leaders should be meeting regularly to assess the impact of the celebrative service on the church and community. Adjustment will almost certainly be necessary. They should be made, even if they involve job descriptions. Improvement here, as everywhere, is a primary goal.

However, it is good to remember that neither Rome nor innovative worship are built in a day. It takes time to install, promote, and fine-tune any church activity. That is especially true of worship, which is central to a majority of members. Endurance may be a key quality. Pastors and staff who initiate change should be committed to staying with the church and the change until it has had time to mature. Here, as elsewhere, the desirability of long pastorates is validated.

In the unlikely event that, even with the best effort possible, celebration really isn't going to work, responsible people should be willing to declare, "We gave it our best shot, but it seems not to be for us right now." Do something else innovative. Improve constantly.

Discovering Spirituality in One Another

One of the ways to revive flagging spirituality that comes to us from the heritage of the Christian church is the use of cells (or small groups) as the bearer of spiritual vitality. The chief advantages are that everyone can be involved and no big changes in other aspects of the life of the church must be made to initiate them. Small groups too are a whole church activity and should receive the full attention of the staff and church during their formation.

The development of the small group, or "cell-based" congregation has been occurring again for the last three decades. Some identify it as the New Testament model of the church. Because the use of cell groups is so often associated with the largest and fastest growing churches there is a tendency to look upon the use of cells as a church growth strategy. However, most of those who use them see cells as a "spiritual growth" design. They are primarily pastoral care units, where the "pastor" is a layperson specifically trained for leadership.

The best-known and most widely used format is the one derived from John Wesley's "class meetings," which began as a way to revive the flagging spirituality (the "spread of scriptural holiness") in the Church of England in the eighteenth century. Some variation of this format is used in most churches that try to devise a comprehensive approach to spiritual renewal.

The class meetings were the smallest unit in a general design which began with the "societies," a collection of persons in the Anglican Church who were seeking greater spirituality. John Wesley said all were welcome who sought to "flee from the wrath to come, and to be saved from their sins." (The society in Bristol had 1,100 members.) The classes were the cornerstone of the whole structure. Composed of five to ten persons, each class had a leader (who could be either a man or a woman and who was not necessarily a "teacher" or even a spiritual guide) charged with the responsibility for inquiring into the spiritual satisfaction and growth of each member. Wesley himself trained all the leaders at first, and only cautiously turned over some of the training to others as the societies grew larger.

The basic format of the weekly meetings was simple. Each week the leader was to "inquire of each member how their souls prosper." There followed testimonies, confessions, questions and admonitions, and the reception of an offering for the poor. (For Wesley there was no separation between the inner and outer holiness.) Wesley wrote in 1748,

> It can scarce be conceived what advantages have been reaped from this little prudential regulation. Many have now happily experienced that Christian fellowship of which they had not so much as an idea before. They began to "bear one another's burdens" and naturally to "care for each other." And "speaking the truth in love" they grew up into him in all things, who is the head, even Christ, from the whole body, fitly joined together, and compacted by that which every joint supplied. (from "A Plain Account of the People Called Methodists" in a letter to the Reverend Mr. Perronet)

At regular intervals the class leader met with the pastor (at first Wesley himself) to provide information on those who were ill or needed further pastoral care.

Ministry through small groups (or cells) has been utilized

for a number of years by a variety of denominations, as well as the independent churches. The employment of laity-led cells not only is one of the most widely used settings for growth in spirituality, it is also readily adaptable to numerous related uses. It may serve as an environment for learning, as an evangelistic tool, as a foundation out of which to do community ministries, or as a vehicle of congregational care. For the purpose of turning the church into a spiritual refreshment center, small groups may be the key.

The pastor and staff will almost certainly be the moving force behind the inauguration and development of cells. They will need to consider the implications for themselves and the congregation very carefully before they embark on that journey. Developing a small group structure in an enduring church is sometimes a massive undertaking.

1. Some very careful research is necessary. Visits with churches that have successful cell organizations in place would be helpful, along with reading books and talking to other leaders.

2. The staff should be engaged in the discussion of the process and its implications for themselves. The establishment of cells will take much of the pastor's time and some staff time for the period of its initiation and for a while thereafter. Duties may have to be restructured, procedures redesigned. Some programs may need to be put on hold for a while. Decisions will have to be made as to which programs staff will continue to administer, and which can be turned over to prepared lay leadership. (That might be an unexpected bonus! We need to do that anyway.) When the cell group process works, it may eventually replace some program structures (and their staff), cutting the total number of staff persons, or drastically changing their roles.

Since the cells will require precedence over everything else the program structures and committees will have to be reduced to the bare minimum and meetings scheduled with care. (Another bonus!)

Unless the pastor decides to do it all (probably not a good idea), the staff will have to be prepared to train and work with leadership for the cells and devote time to the maintenance of the relationship of cells to the body. In some cases staff persons and positions may have to be changed because some roles may not be adaptable to the new system. Some new staff may have to be hired, and some may not wish to participate in the new design and seek other employment. Great sensitivity and compassion are essential to maintaining the gifts administration mode.

3. While later developments may include a number of different kinds of groups with differing purposes, it is better if the primary focus for the first year or two is on spiritual growth and empowerment: (A) Here is where persons may examine and unfold their own spirituality. (B) Here is where leadership for spiritual growth can be developed. (C) Here is where the gifts of persons can best be discovered and cultivated. (D) In these groups the spirituality of the people can be refreshed and strengthened. (E) Pastoral care for everyone is ensured.

4. The most critical stage in the whole process is the selection and training of the laypersons who will lead the groups. *To provide training it will be necessary to develop a very specific "job description," including how the groups are formed, what the agenda will be, and the ways in which the groups relate to the ministry of the whole church.* Each church will have to develop its own procedure. As in the celebration services the content may vary to suit the mission of the body.

A wide range of writers these days are describing the cell leaders as lay pastors and their role as pastoral care. Most successful cell formation includes a "leader's circle" in which the concerns of persons in the groups are shared with the senior pastor or staff at regular intervals by team pastors (leaders or coordinators).

5. Both pastor and staff will need to be committed to

delivering the process to the lay leadership, particularly the board and any program committees or councils. Rationale for the development of a whole church approach to spiritual empowerment will have to be provided (see #3, above), the concept of lay pastoring explained, and assurances given that other important aspects of the life of the church will not be neglected as long as they are needed. During this time no other significant changes should be undertaken, including changes in the worship styles. That may have already occurred or will come later, but not now.

6. Since spiritual growth is the primary focus, groups should not be burdened with extra tasks at first. Limit the effort to Bible reading, prayer, and the sharing of spiritual experiences, the discussion of questions relating to spiritual growth (but not church issues or gossip), and any personal matters for which members would like prayer or support, but including nothing unrelated to the central theme of spiritual growth.

7. As with the Celebration service, there should be constant review of the process by a responsible group of persons, and adjustments made as needed. Leaders should be prepared to stay with the cells for many months.

8. New leaders will emerge from the groups, both for the continuation of the cells, or for ministry groups formed during the spiritual growth process, and for the program activities of the church (such as Sunday school or singles ministries). The intimacy of the small group process is a perfect setting for discovering gifts and leadership abilities. Refreshed leaders may well give the programs new relevance and creative methodology.

Mediating Spirituality Through Special Activities

When staff and members are thinking together about the spiritual impact of the learning and fellowship activities of the local church good things happen for everyone. Spirituality can be mediated through fellowship activities. Youth fellowships, class retreats, recreational programs, family life events, and other gatherings can be turned toward the spiritual without adversely affecting enjoyment. In fact most persons will feel more satisfied with any experience among church members if it is clearly identified with spiritual growth in terminology and procedures that can be understood by the congregation. The staff sets the tone in such environments and can influence the atmosphere in any interaction of persons in church settings. (This does not mean giving the "devotional." Spirituality is deeper than verbosity.) Here, too, the recruitment and training of leaders is crucial. The right gifts for the right times can change lives.

Spirituality may also be mediated through specific activities designed to encourage persons to grow in the faith and practice of Christian living. In addition to the church school, the organization and use of prayer groups, Bible study groups, Koinonia groups, and other sharing and study opportunities can reach a large number of persons who would like an emphasis on spiritual growth. For some, more active involvement is beneficial, with hands-on experiences of discipleship, such as short-term missions, congregational care, or community service. Almost any grouping or activity that is responsive to the gospel may become a resource for spiritual growth if properly conducted. The staff can become the resource persons for the development of these ministries through both personal leadership and training until the laity are able and willing to take responsibility.

Structured spiritual growth programs may be helpful to some. Although not for everybody they do offer options for disciplined study, prayer, and discipleship. Such programs as *Disciple* or *Trinity Bible* studies, *St. Stephens Ministries, Covenant* groups, *Ten Brave Christians, The Emmaus Walk,* or guides in Christian ministry for laity (see the *Ministry of*

God's People by Donna M. Costa or *Each One a Minister* by William J. Carter, both from Discipleship Resources, Nashville). Numerous texts for study groups are available, such as *The Workbook on Spiritual Disciplines* by Maxie Dunnam (Nashville: Upper Room, 1984). Each denomination will have a different list, but many bookstores and resource centers will have a good selection.

One of the strategies for staff could be to select an assortment of these and assign each staff member to become familiar with one or more of them (perhaps involving attendance at an event). Not only would this provide some further growth opportunities for staff, it would enable them to respond when persons seek deeper spiritual insight. The only warning might be that the imposition of one of these on the whole congregation would be an injustice to the variety of the gifts and the differences in spiritual growth needs of persons. They are generally designed for small volunteer groups and work best in that configuration.

Going to the Core

Both the church and its staff will rise or fall on the effectiveness of the ministry of spiritual growth. Everything else depends upon it. Every other ministry will be enhanced and enlarged by it. Unless persons see the spiritual intent and content of the activities of staff and congregation they will respond half-heartedly at best to the rest of the program of the congregation. The search for the core of the life of the church begins with the pastor and staff. When the leadership has come to grips with this dimension every other effort will become easier and more effective.

The keys to opening the door of the spiritual life are different for each person and each setting. Patience and empathy are vital for those who lead in the search, plus an experience of personal spiritual struggle in which the limitations of human aspiration have been seen and the spirit of God has been allowed to enter lives and change presumptions. Going to the core of the spiritual needs of the congregation may well involve going to the core of our own spirituality as a staff first. The development of the spirituality of the staff and that of the congregation will ultimately come from the same source: the presence of God in the Body of Christ and its effect on pastor, staff, and people.

POSTLUDE

Lazarus (Come Forth)

Enlivening the Body

Remember the story of Mary, Martha, and their brother, Lazarus? They were such good friends of Jesus. He seems to have stayed in their home on a number of occasions. During one of those times Martha complained because she was having to do all the work while Mary sat at the feet of Jesus listening to him explain spiritual matters. Jesus reminded Martha that Mary had chosen well: Sometimes we must avoid life's busyness in order to concentrate on learning about the inner life.

The story of this family and the death and resurrection of Lazarus might be a metaphor for the church in the final years of the second millennium.

Lazarus was greatly beloved by Jesus ("He whom you love is ill" [John 11:3]) as is his church ("Christ loved the church and gave himself up for her" [Eph. 5:25]). Lazarus was already well into death, having been in the tomb four days, just as some parts of the church seem to be in decomposition. When Jesus came he was upbraided by Mary and Martha for being so late, but he only said, "Your brother will rise again" (John 11:23). Then Jesus said, "I am the resurrection and the life . . . do you believe this?" Martha, hardly knowing what to do, said, "Yes, Lord, I believe that you are the Messiah, the Son of God, the one coming into the world" (John 11:25-27). She did not know what to say about his powers over death, but she did know that she believed in him. Out of compassion and love (he wept) Jesus raised his dear friend from the grave.

The four points for today's church:

1. For many of us in the church time is running out. We are far into decline, some are already dead.

2. However near we are to death we are still the Body of Christ, and will be, even in decay. There is only one body, of which we are all parts. So we who are in decline are his beloved, too, and deserve ministry even if we seem beyond hope.

3. We must remember that vitality is of the Lord's choosing and may not conform to our notions of liveliness. Rebirth will come when we believe in Jesus Christ enough to throw ourselves open to whatever he calls us to be for his body. Just as Martha, in puzzlement, still declared her confidence in him, so we, also unsure, must put our trust in Jesus if the body is to have the potential for new life!

4. All revitalization is built upon the twin foundations of Martha's hard work and Mary's spiritual attentiveness. One without the other is powerless. The church will be restored to vitality as persons learn to work together in spirituality.

Lazarus reminds us that prospects are never hopeless. Although many have consigned the traditional church to the trash bin of history, a little research will reveal that new life is happening in thousands of settings. Pastors and staffs with a deep sense of spirituality and a will to work together have restored many bodies to vibrant life. As persons seek the will of God for their communities others will follow.

The future of the church is not clouded but bright. As in the past, some sluggish parishes will be renewed, and some of the booming experimental congregations of today will become the enduring churches of tomorrow. In the mainstream, there sometimes may be slowed metabolism and clogged arteries but a pastor, staff, and congregation with skills and spiritual insight can restore them to vitality. Since the larger churches are the most likely to experience growth, the church staff will be central to both spiritual development and physical enlargement. Bringing it to a mature spirituality and full effectiveness is a big step toward restoring the body to life.

BIBLIOGRAPHY

Bauknight, Brian K. *Body Building.* Nashville: Abingdon Press, 1996.

Buttry, Daniel. *Bringing Your Church Back to Life.* Valley Forge, Pa.: Judson, 1988.

Easum, William. *Dancing with Dinosaurs.* Nashville: Abingdon Press, 1993.

Fenhagen, James. *Mutual Ministry.* New York: Seabury, 1977.

Foster, Richard J. *The Celebration of Discipline.* Revised ed. San Francisco: Harper, 1988.

Fowler, James. *Stages of Faith.* San Francisco: Harper & Row, 1981.

Frazee, Randy, and Lyle Schaller. *The Comeback Congregation.* Nashville: Abingdon Press, 1995.

Hutcheson, Richard. *Mainline Churches and the Evangelicals.* Atlanta: John Knox, 1981.

Jones, Ezra Earl. *Quest for Quality in the Church.* Nashville: Discipleship Resources, 1993.

Leas, Speed. *Leadership and Conflict.* Nashville: Abingdon, 1982.

Lee, Harris. *Effective Church Leadership.* Minneapolis: Augsburg, 1989.

McIntosh, Duncan, and Richard Rusbuldt. *Planning Growth in Your Church.* Valley Forge, Pa.: Judson, 1983.

Miller, Herb. *Connecting with God.* Nashville: Abingdon Press, 1994.

Nouwen, Henri. *Creative Ministry.* New York: Doubleday, 1978.

Nuechterlein, Anne Marie. *Improving Your Multiple Staff Ministry.* Minneapolis: Augsburg, 1989.

159

Nuechterlein, Anne Marie, and Celia A. Hahn. *Male-Female Church Staff.* New York: Alban Institute, 1990.

Roberts, Wess. *Leadership Secrets of Attila the Hun.* New York: Warner, 1990.

Schaller, Lyle E. *The Senior Minister.* Nashville: Abingdon Press, 1988.

————. *The Multiple Staff and the Larger Church.* Nashville: Abingdon Press, 1980.

Schutz, William. *Joy.* New York: Grove Press, 1967.

Senge, Peter M. *The Fifth Discipline.* New York: Doubleday, 1990.

Seraydarian, Patricia. *The Professional Church Secretary.* Wheaton, Ill.: Tyndale, 1989.

Shawchuck, Norman, and Roger Heuser. *Leading the Congregation.* Nashville: Abingdon Press, 1993.

Shawchuck, Norman, and Gustave Rath. *Benchmarks of Quality in the Church.* Nashville: Abingdon Press, 1994.

Smith, Donald. *Congregations Alive.* Philadelphia: Westminister Press, 1981.

Steinbron, Melvin. *Can the Pastor Do It Alone?* Ventura, Calif.: Regal, 1987.

Stevens, R. Paul, and Philip Collins. *The Equipping Pastor.* New York: Alban Institute, 1993.

Tillapaugh, Frank. *Unleashing the Church.* Ventura, Calif.: Regal, 1982.

Vaughn, John. *The Large Church.* Grand Rapids: Baker, 1985.

Walton, Mary. *The Deming Management Method.* New York: Putnam, 1986.

Weems, Lovett H., Jr. *Church Leadership.* Nashville: Abingdon Press, 1993.

Westing, Harold. *Multiple Staff Church Handbook.* Grand Rapids: Kregel, 1985.

Wilcox, Mary. *The Developmental Journey.* Nashville: Abingdon, 1979.

Wilson, Marlene. *How to Mobilize Church Volunteers.* Minneapolis: Augsburg, 1983.

Wright, Timothy. *A Community of Joy.* Nashville: Abingdon Press, 1994.